John Rowland West

Parish sermons on the ascension of our Lord

John Rowland West

Parish sermons on the ascension of our Lord

ISBN/EAN: 9783741190186

Manufactured in Europe, USA, Canada, Australia, Japa

Cover: Foto ©Lupo / pixelio.de

Manufactured and distributed by brebook publishing software (www.brebook.com)

John Rowland West

Parish sermons on the ascension of our Lord

PREFACE.

THERE is not *one* of the great events relating to our SAVIOUR which can be overlooked or forgotten by us without some serious loss to our spiritual state. Because *every one* of them forms an essential part of that great work which our SAVIOUR has done and is doing on our behalf, from His descending to His ascending, from His most lowly Nativity in this world, to His most triumphant Ascension into Heaven itself; because also all the Articles of the Christian Faith depend so very intimately on these great events, so that if any one of them be overlooked, we lose at the same time an essential portion of Christian doctrine.

Both for the honour and glory of our LORD

therefore, and for our own sake also, it is our most plain and bounden duty, if we believe in these great events, not only to speak of them privately, and to ponder them in our hearts, but also to celebrate their glory openly and publicly in the Church. We should "*give thanks unto the Lord,*" for all these His mighty works done for our salvation, not only "*secretly among the faithful,*" but as well "*in the congregation.*" The keeping up of the memory of these works is indeed the keeping up of the Christian religion itself, because without these things there is no Christian religion at all.

We read how it was in the Jewish dispensation, by the express command of GOD; the memory of all the great works which GOD had wrought for the children of Israel was kept up by special religious festivals. And we need no new revelation to teach us the propriety and the wisdom and the necessity of this. More therefore now than ever before ought we to celebrate, in yearly Festivals of the Church, the glory of the far greater works now wrought for us, of which those former ones were only the types and figures. Accordingly we do generally observe the days and keep them holy with special worship on which the LORD was born, on which He died, and on which He rose from the dead. But it has become the too common custom to overlook the day on which the same LORD ascended into glory, and sat down on the throne of His kingdom.

Why this is so, it is hard to say; or if any reasons are to be given, they are only full of pain and of shame to us. The fault is not in the least degree with the appointments of the Church. For the Prayer Book contains every possible provision for giving due honour and distinction to the day of the Ascension. There are *Proper Psalms* for the day full of the spirit of prophecy concerning the glories of the Ascension. There are special *Proper Lessons*. There is a special *Collect*, with the *Epistle* and *Gospel*, for the Celebration of the Holy Eucharist, and a proper *Preface* in that chief Service, which last provision is one that is made for only four other seasons of the whole Christian year.

It is a matter therefore very greatly to be

desired, that this evident fault in our present inconsistent practice should be entirely removed from us. For why should we remember the beginning, and then forget the ending? Why should any one come to Church for special worship on Christmas Day, when the LORD from Heaven was laid down in His deep humiliation in the manger at Bethlehem, and not much rather come to Church for special worship on Ascension Day, when the same LORD ascended from Bethany, and was most highly exalted and crowned with glory at the right hand of the Majesty on High? Why should we think of the manger, and of the cross, and then forget the throne of glory? Is it not an open dishonour to our LORD to observe the seasons of His humiliation, and to pass by the grandest season of all, the Festival of the Ascension?

And does not this neglect of the Ascension Day also cause us all to suffer great loss in our own faith? How can we hold the faith in any degree of fulness, as we ought, if we do not dwell on those Articles which depend so entirely on the glorious mystery of the Ascension of our SAVIOUR? Does not this imperfection in our faith show itself very manifestly in our too little appreciation of that work which our ascended LORD is now continually engaged in doing for us? If our LORD had never ascended into Heaven as Man, if He had put off the human nature and were now in Heaven only as He was there before He came down into the world, it would plainly make but little if any difference in the faith of many amongst us. So very greatly are all those Articles of the Faith overlooked which depend on the Ascension of our Incarnate LORD into the glory of the FATHER, there to carry on that work on our behalf which He only began upon earth.

Both then for the due honour of our most holy religion in this world, and for our own great benefit also, it is our bounden duty to do all we can, in our day and generation, to restore the grandest day of the Christian year to its proper observance.

Surely if we celebrate with public worship and with the Holy Eucharist *any* mystery of our faith, we ought to celebrate the exceeding glory of the triumph of the Ascension.

May GOD be pleased to bless this endeavour, all unworthy as it is, and make it subserve towards this end.

The Reader will kindly pardon some degree of repetition and many other imperfections in the following Sermons, as they have been prepared in the midst of the constant occupations of a large Parish.

CONTENTS.

SERMON I.

THE ASCENSION DAY ON EARTH.

                                                                  PAGE

"And He led them out as far as to Bethany, and He lifted up His hands, and blessed them. And it came to pass, while He blessed them, He was parted from them, and carried up into Heaven."—S. Luke xxiv. 50, 51. 1

SERMON II.

THE ASCENSION AND THE SESSION.

"He was received up into Heaven; and sat on the right hand of GOD."—S. Mark xvi. 19. . . . 9

SERMON III.

THE ASCENSION INTO HEAVEN.

"We see JESUS, Who was made a little lower than the Angels, for the suffering of death, crowned with glory and honour."—Heb. ii. 9. 17

SERMON IV.

THE EXALTATION IN HEAVEN ABOVE.

"He raised Him from the dead, and set Him at His own right hand in the heavenly places, far above all principality, and power, and might, and dominion, and every name that is named, not only in this world, but also in that which is to come: and hath put all things under His feet, and gave Him to be the Head over all things to the Church, which is His Body, the fulness of Him that filleth all in all."—Eph. i. 20 to end. 27

SERMON V.

THE CONSUMMATION OF THE GREAT MYSTERY OF GODLINESS.

"Great is the mystery of Godliness: GOD was manifest in the flesh, justified in the Spirit, seen of angels, preached unto the Gentiles, believed on in the world, received up into glory."—1 Tim. iii. 16. . . . 33

SERMON VI.

THE NECESSITY OF THE ASCENSION.

"Nevertheless, I tell you the truth: it is expedient for you that I go away."—S. John xvi. 7. . . 47

SERMON VII.

THE PRESENT LIFE FOR US.

"For if, when we were enemies, we were reconciled to GOD by the death of His SON, much more, being reconciled, we shall be saved by His Life."—Romans v. 10. 57

Contents.

SERMON VIII.

OUR LORD MADE THE HEAD OF THE CHURCH.

PAGE

"And gave Him to be the Head over all things to the Church."—Eph. i. 22. 65

SERMON IX.

THE EXTENSION OF OUR LORD'S PRESENCE.

"He that descended is the same also that ascended up, far above all Heavens, that He might fill all things."—Eph. iv. 10. 77

SERMON X.

THE NEW CONSTITUTION OF THE CHURCH.

"And He is the Head of the Body, the Church."—Col. i. 18. 85

SERMON XI.

THE ONE BODY OF CHRIST.

"There is one Body."—Eph. iv. 4. . . . 91

SERMON XII.

THE NEW KINGDOM OF THE SON OF MAN.

"Verily I say unto you, There be some standing here, which shall not taste of death, till they see the Son of Man coming in His Kingdom."—S. Matth. xvi. 28. 101

SERMON XIII.

THE MINISTRY ON EARTH.

"Then the Eleven Disciples went away unto Galilee, into a mountain where JESUS had appointed them. And when they saw Him, they worshipped Him, but some doubted. But JESUS came, and spake unto them, saying, All power is given unto Me in Heaven and in earth. Go ye therefore, and teach all nations; baptizing them in the Name of the FATHER, and of the SON, and of the HOLY GHOST; teaching them to observe all things whatsoever I have commanded you; and, lo, I am with you alway, even unto the end of the world. Amen."—S. Matth. xxviii. 16—20. ... 107

SERMON XIV.

THE MINISTRY ON EARTH.

"And He gave, some Apostles, and some Prophets, and some Evangelists, and some Pastors and Teachers; for the perfecting of the Saints, for the work of the Ministry, for the edifying of the Body of CHRIST."—Eph. iv. 11, 12. ... 119

SERMON XV.

OUR LORD'S PRIESTHOOD.

"We have a great High Priest, that is passed into the Heavens, JESUS the SON of GOD."—Heb. iv. 10. ... 129

SERMON XVI.

THE FULFILMENT OF THE ANCIENT TYPE.

"By His own Blood He entered in once into the Holy Place."—Heb. ix. 12. ... 137

Contents.

SERMON XVII.

THE PRIESTLY MINISTRATIONS.

"We have such a High Priest, Who is set on the Right Hand of the Throne of the Majesty in the Heavens, a Minister of the sanctuary and of the true tabernacle."—Heb. viii. 1, 2. 149

SERMON XVIII.

THE CONTINUAL MINISTRATIONS.

"He ever liveth to make intercession."—Heb. vii. 25. 157

SERMON XIX.

THE ORDER OF MELCHISEDEK.

"The LORD sware, and will not repent; Thou art a Priest for ever after the Order of Melchisedek."—Psalm cx. 4. 163

SERMON XX.

OUR PRESENT STATE.

"And hath raised us up together, and made us sit together in heavenly places, in CHRIST JESUS."—Eph. ii. 6. 173

SERMON XXI.

THE PROMISE OF OUR ASCENDED LORD.

"To him that overcometh will I grant to sit with Me in My throne, even as I also overcame, and am set down with My FATHER in His throne."—Rev. iii. 21. 181

SERMON I.

THE ASCENSION DAY ON EARTH.

S. Luke xxiv. 50, 51.

"And He led them out as far as to Bethany, and He lifted up His hands, and blessed them. And it came to pass, while He blessed them, He was parted from them, and carried up into heaven."

It was now the fortieth day after the Resurrection; and the space of forty days was the full time of delay. There is a mysterious analogy between the great events of Holy Scripture which are connected with this typical number *forty*. In old time the period of forty days, or of forty years, had marked many such great events; and we can easily distinguish in those events a common character: they were all marked as periods of suffering, or of punishment for sin, or of trial of faith, or of absence from rest. It is the full period of *four tens.* It is, we may say, the type of the period of our probation for the Presence of GOD. It was the period of our LORD'S great temptation in the wilderness; it is the period of His absence from glory after His Resurrection from the dead.

This period was endured by our LORD for our sake, in order that in it He might confirm the faith of His Apostles in the truth of His Resurrection, and that He might give them His final instructions concerning the constitution of His kingdom, and also His final commission to go forth into all nations to preach and to baptize in His Name.

This period was now fulfilled. The time for ascending, the very hour, was indeed now come. The whole work of the LORD upon earth was now quite complete.

He had been laid in the manger, amongst the cattle of the stall; He had lived in privacy, hidden from the world, at Nazareth, "*the son of the carpenter,*" as the world supposed. He had been baptized in Jordan, and made the CHRIST of GOD, receiving, as Man, "*the Spirit without measure.*" He had spoken every parable; He had wrought every miracle; He had suffered every grief; He had shed every tear; He had received every stripe; He had been bruised with every agony; for the perfecting of His obedience He had been nailed upon the Cross; He had made His Soul an Offering for sin; He had bowed His Head in death; He had been laid in the dark and silent tomb; He had gone into Paradise; He had risen again from the regions of the departed.

And He had now shown Himself alive from the dead, by many infallible proofs, to the Apostles whom He had chosen to carry on His work upon earth; He had instructed them with all needful commandments concerning the Mysteries of His Kingdom: and now all was accomplished upon earth; all that the FATHER had given Him to do upon earth was perfectly done; the foundations of His Kingdom were all laid, in pain and labour and blood and death. All was done below.

Why, therefore, should the LORD stay down here any longer? why should the triumph of the Ascension be any longer delayed?

For the joy that was set before Him He had endured the Cross, and now the Crown of Divine Glory was ready. All the heavenly hosts, all the thrones of Heaven were waiting. The exceeding great triumph was now all prepared.

The hour of His departure to the FATHER was therefore now fulfilled. He had stayed here till all below was perfectly finished. Now for the last time He, the LORD GOD Incarnate, walked upon the earth, and led His Apostles out of Jerusalem as far as the Mount of Olives, near to Bethany, passing through those places which had so lately been the scenes of His agonies. And for the last time the LORD JESUS lifts up His hands and blesses His Apostles; making this to be His last action upon earth— a priestly action, *to lift up the hands to bless.*

And whilst the words of His Divine Blessing were yet sounding in their ears, whilst His Holy Hands were yet moving in the act of blessing, behold, the LORD JESUS begins to ascend. His Feet no longer touch the ground, He is parted from His Apostles. He is carried up in exceeding great triumph of more than twelve legions of angels. A bright and dazzling cloud of glory receives Him out of sight of the Apostles. As in a little moment He was gone from their midst. They stood in mute amazement, with straining, dazzled eyes, gazing up into Heaven. But the eye of sense could not pierce through that cloud to see the glory of the exceeding great triumph in Heaven above.

There for a little while they stood, that little flock alone in the world, looking steadfastly upwards, to catch the last glimpse of their ascending LORD.

But He, the Son of Mary, the SON of GOD,

was ascending up far above their mortal sight, higher and higher, even far above all heavens, till He came in our human nature even to the very Throne of the Majesty of the FATHER.

How long the Apostles remained, astonied with an exceeding great astonishment, adoring in silent wonder, filled with awe at this final miracle, hardly daring to speak or to move, we cannot tell. But angels, sent from Heaven in tenderness and love, soon aroused them from their deep amazement. *"Ye men of Galilee,"* they said, *"why stand ye here, gazing up into Heaven? This same Jesus, which is taken up from you into Heaven, shall so come, in like manner, as ye have seen Him go into Heaven."*

These words should dwell in our hearts, and move our whole being, and change our whole life.

Soon shall we behold the same LORD JESUS descending again from Heaven; but then, in the Glory and Power of His Godhead, to be our Judge. Therefore, as the angels would kindly remind us, let us now make it our one only great business to prepare for the tremendous glory of His second appearing, for the open revelation of the power of His kingdom.

But the holy mysteries belonging to His ascension into glory must be received into our hearts by faith, to strengthen us for this very thing. To these, therefore, let us give some of our best attention.

For as the wondering Apostles began to realize the truth that their LORD had actually gone from them into Heaven, what shall we think must have been passing in Heaven itself?

The return of the SON of GOD to the Throne of the FATHER, now no longer GOD only but Man also; the receiving up into glory of GOD manifest in the flesh; the crowning of the LORD JESUS with honour and glory of all the heavenly host; His Session at the right hand of the Throne of the FATHER; how full of unspeakable amazement, how full of heavenly glory, how full of deepest mysteries, how rich in Divine grace and blessing for us!

When the Eternal FATHER brought in the Eternal SON into this world in a condition of exceeding great humiliation, He said, "*Let all the angels worship Him.*"

What, then, must have been the worship of all the heavenly hosts, offered on that day to the same LORD JESUS, now ascending up and passing through all their ranks till He came to the Throne of the FATHER? Then Heaven itself was in some respects changed, for the very Throne of the Eternal FATHER received the Eternal and Co-equal SON *so* as He had never been there before. He carries up our manhood into the highest Heaven. He appears in the Presence of the FATHER now made for ever Man. Then, therefore, was there a new thing in Heaven itself.

Then began to be fulfilled the ancient prophecy, in heavenly truth and reality, in deepest mysteries, " *Behold I create new heavens and a new earth.*"

SERMON II.

THE ASCENSION AND THE SESSION.

S. MARK XVI. 19.

"HE WAS RECEIVED UP INTO HEAVEN; AND SAT ON THE RIGHT HAND OF GOD."

THERE is no Mystery of the Christian Faith more great than this is; there is no Article of the Christian Religion more glorious. Nor are there any doctrines of Divine Revelation more important, than those which depend on the *Ascension* of our LORD into Heaven, and on His *Session* at the right hand of GOD.

In the words of S. Mark there are *two* things revealed to us; first, "*He was received up into Heaven,*" and then, "*He sat on the right hand of God.*"

I. First, "*He was received up into Heaven.*" This is said, of course, in reference to the *human* nature which our LORD had taken. For by virtue of His *Divine* nature our LORD was never absent from Heaven. By virtue of His Godhead, being of one Substance with the FATHER, He was ever present in Heaven. Even when upon earth He could speak of Himself as "*the Son of Man which is in Heaven.*"

But now, by the Mystery of His holy Incarnation, He had come down from Heaven, and had taken upon Him our *human* nature. He had been born of the Blessed Virgin Mary into our human family; He had been laid in the manger at Bethlehem; He had lived in this world a life of humiliation, poverty and suffering; He had endured the pains of death, even the death of the Cross: and now, having arisen from the dead, and having stayed here below for forty days, the time was perfectly fulfilled, the throne of glory was prepared, the Angels lifted up the everlasting doors of Heaven, and the LORD Incarnate was carried up from this world, and received into glory; He was exalted with exceeding great triumph, even unto the throne of the FATHER.

From all eternity indeed, the SON of GOD had lived in the glory of the FATHER, but now *He ascends into Heaven, so* as He had never been there before. He ascends into Heaven *in the human nature,* made now for ever perfect MAN, as well as perfect GOD.

Then therefore there was *a new thing* in

Heaven itself, when *One entered in made in our likeness,* even *the Blessed Son of God made Man.* Then was there a new thing in Heaven itself, when He, the first of all the human family, went up from this world and passed through all the ranks and orders of the heavenly hosts, and was received up into glory, even the glory of the FATHER.

Then was there an exceeding great triumph indeed in Heaven itself, when GOD the Eternal SON, now made for ever Man, returned from His life on earth, bearing in His own human Body the marks of His sufferings here below; when *He* Who had lain in the manger and hung on the Cross, now ascended into the glory of the FATHER, and was crowned in our nature with all honour and worship of all the heavenly host.

II. For now let us consider the second point revealed to us in the text,—the LORD JESUS was not only "*received up into Heaven,*" but farther, "*He sat on the right hand of God.*" We have to consider not only *the Ascension,* but also *the Session* at the right hand of GOD. As S. Paul also writes,—"*Who, for the joy that was set before Him, endured the Cross, despising the shame, and is set down at the right hand of the throne of God.*"

By this expression, "*on the right hand of the*

throne of God," we should understand the place of highest *dignity and glory*, as well as the place of greatest *power and dominion;* and by the word *sitting*, we should understand *that rest and peace* into which our LORD entered, and in which He still *continues to be*, after all His labours and sufferings in this world. After a life on earth of poverty and toil, of abasement and humiliation, of suffering and affliction, *now* the LORD JESUS rests above, in joy unspeakable, in the glory and in the power of the throne of the FATHER, most highly exalted in our human nature, even to the right hand of the Majesty on high.

Thus then, when the MESSIAH ascended into Heaven, that ancient prophecy was fulfilled,—"*The Lord said unto my Lord, Sit Thou on My right hand, until I make Thy enemies Thy footstool.*" Then the LORD CHRIST, the MESSIAH, sat down on the throne of His kingdom, and was crowned with the glory of GOD even in our human nature. Then were fulfilled those words, "*All power is given unto Me in Heaven and in earth.*" Then the LORD JESUS was made both *Lord* and *Christ*.

Thus, therefore, we believe in these two grand Articles of our Creed,—" *He ascended into Heaven; and sitteth at the right hand of God the Father Almighty.*"

Never before had *man* ascended into Heaven. As S. Peter said even of David, "*For David is not ascended into Heaven,*" his body still is in the grave; the bodies of the Saints still sleep in the dust of the earth, and their disembodied spirits still wait in Paradise for the sound of the Archangel's trumpet.

But *the First-fruits* of them that sleep has arisen; *His* body has arisen from the grave, *He* has ascended into Heaven. The Second Adam, the Head of the Mystical Body of the Redeemed, *He* has gone up on high, and passed through the heavens, and has ascended even to the throne of GOD.

One of our race, brethren, one of the same substance and nature with ourselves, Who was born of the Blessed Virgin at Bethlehem, Who lived at Nazareth, Who was crucified on Mount Calvary, even *He* has arisen from the grave, and in the body has ascended, even in our human nature, He has gone in within the veil, our Forerunner, our Divine Head, our SAVIOUR. There He ever lives and reigns, *God manifest in the flesh;* one with the FATHER and the HOLY GHOST, yet still one with us, most high in the glory of GOD the FATHER.

Shall we not then consider these things? Shall we not ponder in our hearts these stupendous mysteries? Shall we not celebrate with all our best affections, and all our most reverent care, *the glory of the supreme triumph*, this infinitely great glory of the Ascension of GOD Incarnate? Is not *this* the grand glory of our race; the Second Adam raised to the throne of GOD; the LORD JESUS sitting at the right hand of the FATHER; *our nature in Him seen* by all the heavenly host *received up into glory*.

He that created all things; *He* that made all the suns and worlds that are scattered in myriads through boundless space, even "*as the sand which is by the seashore, innumerable*," even He Who is the Sovereign LORD of all, is manifest on the throne of GOD, in our human nature, for ever and ever.

Can *any* thing move your hearts, brethren, with deeper thoughts, more amazement, or greater hopes? Oh, ponder this infinitely stupendous Article of your Christian faith more and more in your hearts, *The Son of God ascended into Heaven, made for ever in our nature, living for ever in a human body, manifest in the flesh on the throne of God.*

For what are *the consequences to us* of this Ascension of our LORD, and of His Session on the right hand of GOD? For *what purposes* are these marvellous works of GOD wrought? What are *the effects* to *usward?*

Our LORD ascends, and is glorified, not for

Himself only, but *for our sake*. On His Ascension in our nature into the presence of the FATHER, He receives new gifts of grace, but all *for us* to share in. His new glory in our nature, His new power, His new kingdom, are all *for us and for our salvation*.

He was *born* for us; He *lived* on earth for us; He *died* for us; He *rose again* for us; and now He *ascends* and is *glorified* for us. As S. Paul writes, "*He is gone into Heaven, now to appear in the presence of God for us.*" It is all in order to carry on and to bring to perfection, and to finish *that great salvation for us*, which the LORD began on earth.

Now we may be sure, all the mysteries of CHRIST are opened unto us in all the fulness of the last dispensation. Now that the LORD, the Second Adam, reigns on the throne of His glory, the kingdom of the regeneration has begun.

SERMON III.

THE ASCENSION INTO HEAVEN.

HEB. II. 9.

"WE SEE JESUS, WHO WAS MADE A LITTLE LOWER THAN THE ANGELS, FOR THE SUFFERING OF DEATH, CROWNED WITH GLORY AND HONOUR."

FROM the holy Incarnation of the SON of GOD to His most glorious Ascension, in our Manhood, into the Presence of the FATHER,—*all* indeed, is full of unspeakable mystery and transcendent glory.

But *no event* concerning our SAVIOUR is more glorious, none more full of Christian Instruction, none more intimately connected with our salvation, none more full of joyful hope and comfort, than the Mystery of the Ascension.

"*He ascended into Heaven*" is an Article of our Creed, the very *crown and consummation* of all the preceding ones, the very *top-stone* of the whole building.

Let us then consider a little while to-day this heavenly Mystery, this most great and glorious vision, which is set before us in the text, "*We see Jesus, Who was made a little lower than the Angels, for the suffering of death, crowned with glory and honour.*"

At Christmas-time we see the LORD come down from Heaven, His Divine Glory all hidden, made lower than the angels, born into our Human Family, in an estate of great poverty, in a condition of great humility and weakness, lying, even as a little child, in the manger—in the stable, *beginning* His earthly life of sorrow, shame, and suffering.

On Christmas Day we worship Him, Whom the Heaven of heavens cannot contain, lying on His lowly Throne in the stable.

In Lent we see the LORD JESUS led up of the Spirit into the desert wilderness, fasting for our sake forty days and forty nights; in great humiliation and abasement; in company with the wild beasts; not having where to lay His head; tempted by the great and subtle Tempter; in pain and weakness and affliction; ministered unto, at the end, by angels from Heaven.

O with what sad amazement did those angels then see their Sovereign LORD thus suffering, thus standing in need of their ministrations.

On Good Friday we see the LORD JESUS

lifted up on the Cross; sinking into the dust of death; naked, bleeding, dying; bearing our sins in His own Body on the tree; made the greatest sufferer of all; suffering all He could suffer for us; finishing His life of humiliation here below in the agonies of death, even the death of the Cross; the very Lamb of God slain in Sacrifice for the sins of the world.

On Easter Day we see the Lord risen from the dead, living in His spiritual immortal Body, ready to ascend, but still waiting here below for the space of forty days, until He had given His last instructions to the Apostles concerning His New Kingdom, which they were to set up in all nations.

And *now*, brethren, we arrive at the highest point of all in the Mysteries of God. To-day a more glorious Vision is opened unto us; now we look up into the very glory of the highest Heaven; now we no longer look on this earth; *now* we must lift up our eyes, from the manger, from the wilderness, from the Cross, from the Grave, from the Resurrection. For now we look up into the Heaven of heavens; *now*, by faith, "*we see Jesus*, CROWNED WITH GLORY AND HONOUR"—that same Lord Jesus, whom we crucified here below, now ascended into Heaven, seated in the very glory of the FATHER, in our Manhood, at the right hand of the Majesty on high.

O how inconceivably great the change! From the Manger, from the Cross, from the Grave, even to the Eternal Throne of the FATHER.

This is the vision of glory and of triumph, brethren, which meets us at this season. This is the very crown and consummation of all that had gone before. As S. Paul writes: "*Great is the mystery of godliness; God was manifest in the flesh; justified in the Spirit; seen of angels; preached unto the Gentiles; believed on in the world; received up into Glory.*"

This is the crown and consummation of all the great mysteries of our holy Religion—GOD the SON manifest in the flesh, *received up into glory;* GOD the SON made man *crowned with glory and honour.*

Who can conceive, brethren—who can conceive—*the exceeding great triumph* of all the Heavenly Host on this Ascension of the LORD JESUS into glory? Who can describe *the reception* of the Incarnate SON of GOD into the Heaven of Heavens? Who can think properly of that *entering-in* of the LORD JESUS—when the everlasting doors of Heaven were lifted up, and He ascended from this world, and passed

The Ascension into Heaven. 21

through all the ranks and armies of the Heavenly Host, and was exalted far above all the powers and principalities—all the thrones and dominions of Heaven—even till He came, in our manhood, to the very Throne of the FATHER—when that ancient prophecy was fulfilled,—"*The Lord said unto my Lord, Sit Thou on My right hand, till I make Thy foes Thy footstool.*"

Then surely was all Heaven moved, when the Eternal SON of GOD, who had been made a little lower than the angels, for the suffering of death, now returned from this world, and ascended into Heaven in our nature, made Man for ever, and sat down at the right hand of the Majesty on high, and was crowned, as Man, with all Glory and Honour.

Then began that new song, never heard before in Heaven, sung by all the Heavenly Host, in exceeding great triumph,—"*Worthy is the Lamb that was slain, to receive power, and riches, and wisdom, and strength, and honour, and glory, and blessing.*"

Then, instead of the lowly *manger* here upon earth, the LORD JESUS received *the Throne of the Father.* Instead of the *cattle* standing by, He received *all the armies of Heaven,* ten thousand times ten thousand, in all their excellency of strength. Instead of poverty upon earth beneath, He received all the riches of the eternal Heaven above. Instead of humiliation and abasement, all highest honour and exaltation. Instead of the contempt and rebuke of sinful men, the worship of all the Heavenly Host, the adoration of all the creations of Heaven. Instead of the bloody Cross and the Crown of thorns, the Throne of the Majesty of GOD and the Crown of eternal glory. Instead of the reed of scorn, the Sceptre of an everlasting Kingdom.

Who, brethren, shall venture to speak or to think of the exceeding glory of *that Crown* with which the SON of GOD was then crowned, in the Human Nature, on the Throne of the FATHER?

If even, for every saint, there is prepared a crown of glory that fadeth not away, which he shall receive from the LORD when his trial is done,—*what* (must we suppose) *what* must be the infinite splendour and the supreme glory of *that Crown* which was prepared for the King of Saints Himself?

But all the glory, all the triumph of the Ascension, is briefly expressed in these words of Holy Scripture,—"*He was received up into Heaven, and sat down at the right hand of the Majesty on high; crowned with glory and honour.*"

And *there*, therefore, *we* now, by faith, *see Him*, in all the perfections of the Manhood and in all the perfections of the Godhead, one with us, one with GOD, reigning in glory above on the Throne of the FATHER. *There* we now see the *Lord Jesus*, crowned with glory and honour, in the very Majesty of the Godhead, yet still in our Manhood.

Let us now conclude by very briefly calling to mind *one* of the *many* doctrines which follow from the Ascension of our LORD.

How *full of comfort*, how *full of strong consolation* it is to every true believer to know that, in the very power and majesty of the highest Heaven, there is *One* Who has our human nature, *One* Who still calls us *His brethren*, *One* Who knows by His own experience here below the trials, the difficulties, the sorrows, the temptations, which surround us all in this world.

The SAVIOUR Whom we believe in, Whom we worship, Whom we trust in, Whom, may we say, we desire to love, even He has lived here upon earth in our nature; He has lived in an humble and lowly home, even in the cottage of a carpenter; He has lived in obscurity; He has tasted the hardships of poverty; He has felt the sinless affections and infirmities of our human nature; He has felt a mother's love;

He has learned obedience by the things which He suffered; He has borne our griefs and carried our sorrows in His heart; He has wept at the open grave of a friend; He has Himself sunk into the helplessness of death; He has been buried in the sepulchre.

And now He has carried up that same human nature, *that same human heart* which He had here below, which can be touched with a feeling of all our infirmities, which knows all our sorrows; He has carried up *that same human heart* into the highest heaven, even unto the Throne of infinite power and glory, where He is now *able to save to the uttermost*, seeing that He now ever liveth, in the Presence of the Father, as our great High Priest, to minister on our behalf, to make intercession for us.

There He takes a perfect interest in every one of us, even in His humblest and weakest disciple; there He feels for every one of us; there He ministers for every one of us, sending us continually the Holy Ghost, the Spirit of grace, to sanctify, to strengthen, to comfort, to teach, to save every willing soul.

O look up then, brethren, into the height of Heaven; see there in glory One Who has your Nature; *One* Who perfectly loves you, Who made you by His Power, Who redeemed you by His Blood; *One* Who can feel for you; *One* Who intercedes for you; *One* Who will lift you up from the dust of death, and cause you to ascend into Heaven also, and give you a share in His Own Joy and Glory, that where He is there you may be also,—if you will indeed now *believe* in Him, and *follow* Him, and *keep His words.*

SERMON IV.

THE EXALTATION IN HEAVEN ABOVE.

EPH. I. 20 TO END.

"HE RAISED HIM FROM THE DEAD, AND SET HIM AT HIS OWN RIGHT HAND IN THE HEAVENLY PLACES, FAR ABOVE ALL PRINCIPALITY, AND POWER, AND MIGHT, AND DOMINION, AND EVERY NAME THAT IS NAMED, NOT ONLY IN THIS WORLD, BUT ALSO IN THAT WHICH IS TO COME: AND HATH PUT ALL THINGS UNDER HIS FEET, AND GAVE HIM TO BE THE HEAD OVER ALL THINGS TO THE CHURCH, WHICH IS HIS BODY, THE FULNESS OF HIM THAT FILLETH ALL IN ALL."

HERE is revealed unto us the supreme exaltation of our LORD after His Resurrection from the dead. Here is a description of the glory and power which GOD the FATHER gave unto our LORD when He ascended into His Presence in our human nature.

What event more great or glorious can ever occupy our thoughts than this Ascension of the

LORD JESUS into the Power and Glory of the FATHER.

Let us now consider the terms in which S. Paul here speaks of it.

"*God set Him at His own right hand.*" That ancient prophecy which the HOLY GHOST spake by the mouth of His servant David was then fulfilled: "*The Lord said unto my Lord, Sit Thou on My right hand.*"

The LORD JEHOVAH, GOD the FATHER, said unto David's LORD and SON, the MESSIAH,— "*Sit Thou on My right hand,*" when He ascended up from this world, and appeared before the Presence of the FATHER, no longer *God only*, but now for ever made *Man*.

In another Epistle S. Paul writes: "*To which of the angels said He at any time, Sit on My right hand?*"

To no one of them, but only to the LORD JESUS, did the FATHER ever say, "*Sit Thou on My right hand,*" and this He did *when He ascended into Heaven in our human nature.*

This expression, then, signifies to us that on the Ascension our LORD received of the FATHER the highest exaltation, both in glory and in power. As GOD, indeed, our LORD could not be said to *receive* anything; but we must remember that on this Ascension our LORD appears as *Man* also. It is *in the human nature,* as *Man*, that the LORD our Redeemer is most highly exalted on His Ascension.

This exaltation of the Incarnate Word is further described in the passage before us; it is "*far above all principality, and power, and might, and dominion, and every name that is named, not only in this world, but also in that which is to come.*"

Our LORD is exalted, not simply "*above*," but "*far above*" all the thrones and powers of Heaven. The height of our LORD's exaltation is *above* all created powers, even *far above* them. He is exalted into the very glory of the FATHER. He sits down, in our human nature, at the right hand of the Majesty on high, even in the very Throne of the FATHER.

"*All things are put under His feet;*" all things that are great and glorious, whether in Heaven or in earth, all created powers, by whatever name called, either here below, or there above, *all* are *put under* our ascended LORD. "*All power is given unto Him in Heaven and in earth.*" He is given to be, even as Man, "*King of kings and Lord of lords.*"

That same Jesus, Who once was born of the Blessed Virgin, who once was laid in the manger in the stable; who once lived here below, a Man of sorrows; who once was nailed upon the Cross: who once was dead and buried;—has now been raised up from the dead by the glorious power of the Godhead, and exalted into the glory of the FATHER, far above all the thrones of Heaven.

S. Paul, having thus described the supreme exaltation of the LORD JESUS above all created powers, proceeds to reveal to us that our LORD, on His Ascension, was given to be, in particular, "*the Head over all things to the Church.*"

Here let us call to mind that just as the LORD Himself received *a New Name*, even "*Jesus*," when He was made Man; even so the *Church of God* receives *a New Name* when the LORD Incarnate is glorified. This *New Name* is revealed to us only by S. Paul. It occurs, first of all, and only, in his Epistles. It is, "*The Body of Christ.*" As it is here— "*And gave Him to be the Head over all things to the Church, which is His Body.*"

Before the Incarnation of the SON of GOD, and *before* His Ascension, the Church never was, and never could have been, "*the Body of Christ.*" It never was, and never could have been, "*the Fulness of Christ.*"

But on the Ascension of the Incarnate SON into the glory and power of the FATHER, *then* the LORD was given to be the Head of a new mystical body; *then* men here below began to be "*added to the Lord*," incorporated into the mystical Body of CHRIST, made members of a New Divine Head.

Now, therefore, we have the gift of Regeneration, a gift which never *was* and never *could* have been given to the saints of former ages, before the LORD Himself was made Man. Now we are baptized into that Body of which the ascended and glorified LORD is Himself the Head. Now we are made members, in one Body, with CHRIST, our Divine life-giving Head.

These new titles which are here given to the Church—"*the mystical Body of Christ,*" and "*the Fulness of Him Who filleth all in all*"—are sufficient to teach us that the Church stands in a closer relationship to the LORD Incarnate than any other of the powers or glories of creation.

The Church is *the Body of Christ, the Fulness of the Incarnate Lord.* It is the New Creation; it is the Bride of CHRIST, whom He came down to seek for in this world; whom He *makes one with Himself,* for whom He gave even Himself. As baptized into this one Body of CHRIST, we are united to our risen and ascended Head, the Incarnate SON of GOD; we are made members of the Second Adam, reigning above in the power and glory of the FATHER; from whom is derived unto us the power of an immortal life, the virtue of whose Resurrection is even now, in *some* measure, communicated unto us.

How great, then, is our honour and dignity! How great our glory, even *now*, already united in one body with our *Divine Head, the glorified Jesus!* How full of immortal glory, *our Hope!* To be raised up from the dead, even as *He* was, by the mighty power of Him who is our Resurrection and our Life; and then to ascend up into His Presence, to behold His glory, to be made partakers of His eternal kingdom.

For this is the amazing promise He hath sent us since His Ascension: "*To him that overcometh will I grant to sit with Me in My throne; even as I also overcame, and am set down with My Father in His throne.*"

SERMON V.

THE CONSUMMATION OF THE GREAT MYSTERY OF GODLINESS.

1 TIM. III. 16.

"GREAT IS THE MYSTERY OF GODLINESS: GOD WAS MANIFEST IN THE FLESH, JUSTIFIED IN THE SPIRIT, SEEN OF ANGELS, PREACHED UNTO THE GENTILES, BELIEVED ON IN THE WORLD, RECEIVED UP INTO GLORY."

IN this passage of Holy Scripture are briefly contained the great miracles of GOD wrought for the salvation of fallen man. Here is briefly summed up, in six short sentences, the several parts of the great mystery of Godliness, the sum and substance of the Christian Revelation. Each several part is indeed itself a great mystery; just as each star in a constellation of glory is itself a great sun; each part must be received by us through faith in Divine Revelation; for the great mystery of Godliness is altogether above and beyond mere human reason, although not contrary to it nor destructive of it.

1. Let us begin with that part of the stupendous mystery which is the foundation of all the rest, namely, "the manifestation of GOD in the flesh;" in other words, the Incarnation of the SON of GOD. This is the first part, the beginning, the foundation of the whole mystery of CHRIST, "GOD manifest in the flesh." The Second Person in the One Eternal Godhead, He Who was in the beginning with GOD, being GOD of GOD, of one Substance with the FATHER, the Creator of all worlds, the Maker of angels, the Sovereign LORD of all Creation, even He, so great, so glorious, the Very GOD Who made us, in amazing condescension, in boundless compassion and love towards us in our fallen state, willingly undertook to be our SAVIOUR. For this end, in the order of Divine wisdom, it was needful that He should be *made Man;* so that taking upon Himself our manhood He might become to us *a Second Adam,* a new Divine Life-giving Head, uniting us to Himself, and so conveying to us eternal life.

This is the beginning, the foundation of our salvation, even the Incarnation of the Eternal SON of GOD, the manifestation of One Who is GOD in our human Nature. This is the miracle of miracles, the mystery of mysteries, the very wonder of eternity, the glory of all glories for us, that the Second Person of the eternal Trinity is manifest in our nature, made for ever Man.

O how infinitely has GOD loved us, that the Eternal SON should be thus made in our likeness and nature. Here is the strong and glorious foundation of our salvation; here is the link that joins us on to the very throne of GOD, yea, even to GOD Himself; here is the grand mystery of our Christian faith, the infinite great glory of the human race, that GOD the SON is for ever Man.

2. Next, S. Paul says, "justified in the Spirit." To understand this part of the great mystery of Godliness, we must call to mind that when GOD was manifested in our nature upon this earth, He was manifested at first in the midst of weakness, poverty, humility, and affliction. He made Himself of no reputation; He laid aside the Sceptre of the Universe; He put off the Crown of Glory; He was manifested in meekness and lowliness, in the weakness of the flesh.

Call to mind, brethren, for a moment, the low estate of GOD Incarnate, at first, in this world: born in a stable, laid in a manger, visited by poor shepherds, employed in a lowly trade, attended by poor fishermen, exposed to hunger and thirst, weariness and nakedness, misunderstanding and contempt; and, at last, weighed down beneath His burden, suffering unspeakable agonies, crowned with thorns, bleeding with the cruel scourging, spit upon by sinful men, crucified in weakness, dying in the lowest abasement, sunk down into the deepest abyss of affliction. Thus would GOD, when manifest in the flesh, be manifested in all weakness.

Nevertheless, in the midst of all this weakness of the flesh, He was *justified in or by the Spirit*. That is to say, He was proved to be GOD, even in the midst of this weakness, in or by the working of the Eternal Spirit. His Nativity was celebrated by a multitude of the heavenly Host. At His Baptism, the heavens were opened, and the Eternal Spirit descended, and the Voice of the FATHER was heard upon earth. His Divine Nature was after that manifested by plain testimonies and mighty operations of His co-essential Spirit; for the blind saw, the deaf heard, the lame walked, the dumb spake, the lepers were cleansed, and the dead were raised to life again. Thus, by mighty signs and miracles, by His own Resurrection from the dead, by His visible Ascension into heaven, and by the coming of the HOLY GHOST ten days afterwards according to His promise, our SAVIOUR, although manifested in the flesh at first in great humility and weakness, yet was "justified in or by the Spirit," and thus proved to be God, the Eternal Son Incarnate, the very Messiah, God with us.

3. Next, the Apostle says, "seen of Angels." This is indeed no small part of the great mystery, that He Who is the God of all Spirits should be *seen* by those heavenly Spirits *clothed in our flesh*. The holy angels beheld their Maker made a little lower than themselves. They saw God living as Man here below. What an amazement to the holy angels, to behold Him Who reigned above in the glory of the Father and of the Holy Ghost, now reduced to the poverty and the weakness of our humanity. They had seen His infinite glory above, and now they see His amazing humiliation here below.

Thus, they saw the Lord, when He was born at Bethlehem and laid in the manger borrowed from the cattle. They saw Him living for so many years in a willing obscurity in Nazareth. They saw Him in the wild desert, where no other creatures were near Him, save the wild beasts and the evil spirits; there they saw Him weak with fasting, suffering temptation; and when the trial was ended, they came and ministered unto the sad necessities of their Sovereign Lord God. They saw God manifest in the flesh, also, in the garden of Gethsemane in His grievous agony; for in that hour "there appeared an angel from heaven, strengthening Him." Then He Who upholds all things by the word of His power, Himself become the greatest Sufferer of all, received comfort from an angel.

But more gladly did the holy angels minister unto Him, when He arose from the sepulchre, the Conqueror of death and hell; and still more gladly, when the Day of exceeding great joy and triumph came, and the doors of heaven were opened, and the Son of Man ascended to His throne. Then the multitude of the heavenly Host saw the Eternal SON manifest in the flesh enter into His glory, received up even to the throne of the FATHER, and crowned in our human nature with the crown of eternal glory, even with the glory of the FATHER.

4. But, fourthly, the Apostle writes, "preached unto the Gentiles." Here is that mystery of CHRIST, the mystery of the Epiphany, which had been so long hidden from the saints in the secrets of Divine wisdom. Of old time, as it is written, "In Judah was GOD known, His Name was great in Israel" only; whilst we, sinners of the Gentiles, sat in darkness and the shadow of death, without GOD in the world, strangers from the Covenant of Promise, aliens from the commonwealth of Israel. (Ephes. ii. 12.)

But, on the coming of the Messiah, at the Manifestation of GOD in the flesh, this wall of partition between Jew and Gentile was broken down and taken away; *now* the grace of GOD which bringeth salvation hath appeared unto *all* men; now the ascending SAVIOUR commands that the Gospel should be preached to every single creature in *all* nations; now the HOLY GHOST is given to *all* flesh; now *all* are admitted, without the least distinction of race or nation, into the one Body of CHRIST, on the same conditions of repentance and faith, everywhere. Now the Church has become *Catholic*. Now the Name of the LORD is "great among the Gentiles." This mystery, kept hid for so many ages, is now openly revealed, and we, who were not a people, are now the people of the LORD. Now GOD has "made the barren woman," (that is, the Gentile Church,) "to keep house, and to be a joyful mother of children." Now, on the Ascension of the LORD GOD Incarnate to the throne of His kingdom, we sing with more understanding, "GOD is the King of all the earth; GOD reigneth over the heathen; the princes of the people are joined unto the people of the GOD of Abraham."

5. The next point in the great Mystery of Godliness is, that GOD manifest in the flesh should be "believed on in the world."

So poor, and lowly, and weak was the LORD's first Advent in the flesh, that it would have been scarcely any wonder at all if the world had entirely overlooked Him and utterly disregarded Him; for the world is led by the outward appearance.

That One, therefore, so born, so living, so dying, should be *believed on in the world* as the Eternal SON of GOD, is no small part of this heavenly mystery. Had GOD been manifested in all His own Majesty, in the glory of His Divine Nature, attended with legions of angels and archangels, how ready would the world have been to profess belief in Him and to follow Him! But being manifested in the greatest humility, and requiring the greatest self-denial in all His followers, it is a marvel of Divine grace and power that they should have been convinced of His Deity, that any should have believed on Him as the SON of GOD manifest in the flesh, and ventured all on His word, and gloried in nothing but in the excellency of the knowledge of Him.

6. But the last and the most glorious part of the great mystery of godliness yet remains. In all the former parts, great indeed is the mystery; but *that* which closes them is the most great and glorious one,—even this, that GOD manifest in the flesh should be " received up

into glory." This is the end, the crown, the consummation of the whole: "GOD the SON, made for ever Man, received up into the glory of the FATHER."

Who of us can anyhow conceive aright of the exceeding glory of that reception of the Incarnate SON of GOD? Then He was most highly exalted in our human nature; all power was given unto Him in heaven and in earth. He was constituted the Head of the Church, which is now His mystical Body. He was enthroned on the throne of His everlasting kingdom; He entered into His glory; He was crowned, in our human nature, with the glory of the FATHER, amidst the exceeding great triumph of all the heavenly hosts.

Whether of the two was greater, we know not; for the angels to see GOD manifest in the flesh here below, in a condition below themselves; or, for them to see Him manifest in our human nature, ascending up into glory, carried above all the thrones of the highest cherubim, enthroned on the very throne of the FATHER. But surely, if the joy of heaven admits of any increase, then it rose to the highest pitch, when the celestial hosts beheld the stupendous triumph of the Ascension entering in, coming up within the uplifted gates of heaven; when they saw the Eternal SON of

GOD made Man, after so painful a life in this world, after so dreadful a battle with the powers of evil, "received up into glory," and sitting down at the right hand of the Majesty on high. Who of us can think rightly of that Crown of Infinite Majesty with which He was then crowned? Who of us can anyhow speak rightly of the amazing change, from the stable, cross, and grave, to the very Throne of GOD Most High?

And herein, brethren, lies all our safety, all our hope, all our glory; that He Who is our SAVIOUR is thus most highly exalted; that He Who is the Head of the Church has ascended to the throne of the FATHER; that He Who is One with us ever lives to intercede for us in the Presence of the FATHER; that our life is in Him.

Thus, then, have we briefly considered the six parts of the great mystery of godliness, in the order of the text. The stupendous mystery begins with *God manifest in the flesh* here below, in a condition of great humiliation. Then the power of His Godhead is revealed through the mighty working of the Eternal Spirit. The holy angels desire to look into the great mystery; they behold the Incarnate SON of GOD laying the foundations of His everlasting kingdom in toil and pain, in lowliness, suffering, and death. The great mystery is revealed unto the Gentiles, that *all* men may see the salvation of GOD. It then begins to be believed on even in this world; and so marvellous a faith raises the believer to newness of life. And finally, the Apostle concludes the mystery with the exceeding great triumph of the Ascension, when GOD manifest in the flesh was "received up into glory."

Let us now make two further reflections on the whole. First, let us see how good and profitable it is that the Church on earth should commemorate these chief events in our SAVIOUR's life, from His Incarnation to His Ascension, in holy Festivals from year to year, even till He comes again in His glory. What else, indeed, is worth a moment's thought or trouble in comparison of these things? Let us therefore never fail to assemble ourselves together to worship and glorify GOD on these the greatest of all possible occasions. This is surely required at our hands, if we have any faith and any love towards our SAVIOUR, any regard for His honour and glory in the world, and any right desire for the true advancement of our own souls in the saving knowledge of the mysteries of His kingdom. And here let me particularly put you in mind of Ascension-day,— the day on which the LORD Incarnate ascended into glory. Why should we remember the day of the LORD's Nativity, and not rather the day of His Ascension? Why should we regard the beginning and not rather the ending of the stupendous mystery of godliness? Surely, if anything is plain, it is this; that we ought to honour with all the honour we can, we ought to celebrate, with the greatest care and reverence possible, *all* the mighty miracles that GOD has wrought for us, *all* the great events in our SAVIOUR's life; and very specially indeed, the crowning point of all, the very consummation of the whole mystery, *the glorious Ascension of our Incarnate Lord.* If we forget this, we forget the grandest part of all; we cannot surely understand our faith aright; we must be led merely by the custom of the world, not by true principle.

Lastly, let us think with ourselves, *what is the effect* of the great mystery of godliness upon us? Does it make any real impression upon our minds? Does it make any real difference in our lives? or are we not hearing it only as we hear some pleasant tale?

What effect upon us have all the wonders that GOD has wrought for us? Shall all heaven be so concerned for our salvation, and we live in careless unconcern about it? Shall the very Throne of GOD be moved for us, and we live on in an idle dream? Oh, let us be well assured that, if our whole being is not deeply stirred and changed by the great mystery of godliness, we are sinking quietly, but surely, into hell. Oh let us give earnest heed to the exceeding great Articles of the Christian Faith, now that there is time for them to produce in us their proper effects and fruits.

SERMON VI.

THE NECESSITY OF THE ASCENSION.

S. JOHN XVI. 7.

"NEVERTHELESS, I TELL YOU THE TRUTH: IT IS EXPEDIENT FOR YOU THAT I GO AWAY."

How often we do not understand what is really most expedient for us. How often we misjudge the dealings of GOD with us. How often we mourn for blessings removed, when, if we did but see all that GOD sees, we should rather praise Him, for what will prove in the end to be really most profitable and expedient for us.

The disciples were greatly troubled—they thought it would be a great loss to them—when the LORD plainly declared that He was about to leave them. But our LORD *assured them* that it was *expedient for them* that He should go away; *He assured them* that they should be the *gainers*.

And not only for them, but for us also, and for the whole Church, it was expedient that the LORD JESUS should ascend into Heaven.

Let us endeavour to consider in some degree *four very great reasons* why it was most highly expedient for the whole Church that the LORD JESUS should ascend.

I. The first reason is this—that *the Lord Jesus might Himself be glorified.*

He had humbled Himself exceedingly. He had emptied Himself of His glory, and had been *made Man* here below. He had submitted Himself, *as Man*, to a life of weakness and of poverty, and of reproach, and of suffering, even unto death. He had endured even the death of the Cross. "*Wherefore* (S. Paul writes) *God also hath highly exalted Him, and given Him a Name which is above every Name.*"

For, on our LORD's Ascension, in our nature, into Heaven, that most ancient prophecy of David was fulfilled, "*The Lord said unto my Lord, Sit Thou on My right hand.*" Then, "*All Power was given unto Him, of the Father, both in Heaven and in earth;*" GOD gave Him to be "*Head over all things to the Church.*" Therefore, S. Paul writes,—"*We see Jesus, who was made a little lower than the Angels, for the suffering of death*, CROWNED WITH GLORY AND HONOUR."

The Necessity of the Ascension.

He, Who had been born of the Blessed Virgin Mary, and had been laid in the lowly manger; *He* Who had lived a life of poverty, rebuke, and suffering, here below; *He* Who had died upon the bloody Cross; even THAT SAME JESUS, the *Man of Sorrows here below,*—now we see Him, enthroned above on the Throne of the FATHER; now we see Him crowned with glory and honour for ever. And this, we must consider, is *for us.* The LORD JESUS is thus exalted, empowered, and glorified, for our unspeakable benefit, as our SAVIOUR, our King, our new Divine Head, our Great High Priest. It is all our gain. It is for our salvation and eternal glory. This glory of the Ascension is for us also to enter into.

II. Secondly, brethren, it was expedient that the LORD JESUS should ascend into Heaven, in order that, as S. Paul writes, "*He might fill all things;*" "*He that descended is the same also that ascended up far above all Heavens, that He might fill all things.*"

Here, we must bear in mind, that *as God,* our LORD already *filled all things* with His Presence. For, as it is written, "*In Him and by Him all things consist.*" But, as *made Man,* our LORD was present *before* His Ascension *only* in *one* place *at a time.* His human Body was subject to the same laws of nature as *ours* are; it could not be present everywhere. But, *after* the Ascension, when that *natural Body* had been made a *spiritual Body*, and had been *glorified, then* the Presence of the Lord began to *fill all things*. So that now, the Lord Christ, not simply and only as *God*, but as *God Incarnate*, fills the whole Body of the Church. Now the Presence of the glorified Manhood of our Lord is extended, through the Presence of the Holy Ghost, throughout the whole Church. And the gift of membership in this mystical Body of the Second Adam, our new Divine Head, our Quickening Spirit, the Incarnate Word, is necessary to our very Salvation. For by this membership it is that we receive our new Life in Christ.

III. In the *third* place let us consider that it was expedient that the *Lord Jesus* should ascend, in order that He might enter into His Office, *as Priest*, in the true Sanctuary above, in the very Presence of the Father.

On earth beneath our Lord had been called, by God the Father, at His Baptism, to be *the Christ*, that He might be our *Prophet*, our *Priest*, our *King*. But as our Lord did not begin His regal office, so He did not begin to execute the office of His Priesthood, in all its heavenly power and glory, so as to render effectual all that He had done on earth below, until He ascended and appeared before the Presence of the FATHER in our nature in Heaven above. *Then* He entered in, within the vail, *our true Aaron*, into the true Holy of holies, carrying in with Him, and presenting before the true Mercy-Seat of GOD, *not* the Blood of the Jewish sacrifices, but "*His own Blood*,"—offering within the vail the infinitely precious Blood, *His Own Sacrifice.*

And who can tell, brethren, HOW EXPEDIENT it is that we should *thus* "*have a Priest*," ever ministering for us at the very Heavenly Altar, in the very Presence of the FATHER.

Now He ever liveth, our true and great High Priest, ministering for us, within the vail, showing forth the one infinite eternal sacrifice, and interceding thereupon on our behalf—a merciful and compassionate High Priest—Who having suffered in the flesh Himself, can be touched with human sympathy for us, in all our daily struggles, with all the manifold evils of this present world. *There*, at the right hand of the Throne of GOD, our ascended LORD ever now appears "*for us;*" *there* He now ever executes His Priestly Office *on our behalf*, able to save to the uttermost,—applying to us all the benefits of His Sacrifice, sending us help from His holy Place.

Now, therefore, we have a Mediator and an

Advocate in the very Presence of the FATHER; One made like unto us; Who is the continual propitiation for our sins; ever taking away the sins of His people, and sending them grace, mercy, and peace.

IV. Lastly, it was greatly expedient that our LORD should ascend to the FATHER in our nature, in order that *the full ministration of the Spirit might begin.*

In the *former* dispensations, indeed, the HOLY GHOST had been given in *some* degrees and measures—but it was not until the SON of GOD had become Incarnate, and had ascended as Man into the Presence of the FATHER, and had been made our new Divine Head, that the HOLY GHOST was given in all the fulness of His abiding indwelling Presence. As it is written, " *The Holy Ghost was not yet given, because that Jesus was not yet glorified.*"

In the Order of the Divine will it was necessary that the LORD Incarnate should ascend, and be made *the Head of the Church*, which is *His Body*, before the HOLY GHOST should be *poured out upon all flesh* in all the fulness of His grace. But ten days after the Ascension the LORD poured out this new gift upon His Church below. Then, *on the Coming of the Holy Ghost*, the final dispensation of the grace of GOD began. Then, old things passed away;

The Necessity of the Ascension. 53

all things were made new. Then the New Kingdom of Heaven was opened upon earth to all believers. Then began the new creation of man in CHRIST JESUS, the second Adam. Then the Church began to be "*the Body of Christ—the fulness of Him Who now filleth all in all.*" Then began "*the last days,*" the ministration of the Spirit, the dispensation of the HOLY GHOST, in which we are now living.

Such, then, brethren, are four exceedingly great reasons for which it was expedient for the whole Church that the LORD JESUS should ascend into the Presence of the FATHER. All things were waiting for that infinitely great and glorious event. *All* would have been fruitless without the Ascension of our LORD into Heaven. But then, the Incarnate LORD, the LORD JESUS, even He Who had laid in the manger and died on the Cross,—even that same JESUS,—was exalted into the Power and Glory of the FATHER. Then He began to be the Head of the Church, so that the Church is now *His mystical Body*, filled everywhere with His Presence, so that it is "*the fulness of Him Who filleth all in all.*" Then He began to execute the office of a *Priest* in the very Presence of the FATHER for us. And then, also, He obtained new gifts for us, of unspeakable grace, even that the *Lord God, the Holy Ghost,* should come down from Heaven to dwell not only *with us*, but *in us*, at Whose coming the kingdom of Heaven was opened upon earth—into which we enter at our Baptism.

Let us often consider with ourselves these great and glorious mysteries of the kingdom of CHRIST, in the midst of which we are now placed.

And let us now make one practical application of these heavenly mysteries. If we had been living *before* the Incarnation of the SON of GOD, and *before* His Ascension into Heaven in our nature, and *before* the coming of the HOLY GHOST,—GOD would have looked for *such good fruits* from us as corresponded to the gifts of His grace which we then should have possessed. But being members of the *Church of Christ*—living, as we now are, in the *ministration of the Spirit*, members of our *new Divine Head;* fed with the spiritual Food of His most *precious Body and Blood;* our very bodies made *temples of the Holy Ghost;* possessing, as we now do, *higher* and *better* gifts of grace than any of the Saints ever did before; nothing more or greater coming to us but only the tremendous glories of the second Advent of the LORD,—what manner of persons ought we to be in all holy conversation and godliness! what *excellent fruits ought we to be bringing forth unto God!* Let us consider that in the last great day *we* must be judged by the *highest standard* of all. Of *us*, surely, GOD is now expecting *the best fruits.*

What, then, are we the better for our higher gifts? What are the more excellent and more abundant fruits of our *repentance towards God*, and of our *Faith towards our Lord Jesus Christ?*

SERMON VII.

THE PRESENT LIFE FOR US.

ROMANS V. 10.

"FOR IF, WHEN WE WERE ENEMIES, WE WERE RECONCILED TO GOD BY THE DEATH OF HIS SON, MUCH MORE BEING RECONCILED, WE SHALL BE SAVED BY HIS LIFE."

THESE words of Holy Scripture should serve to teach us, that we should not confine our thoughts, concerning our SAVIOUR, to His Life and Death in this world; but that we should, *even much rather*, carry them on to His present Life in Heaven. The Apostle most plainly declares that our salvation is closely connected, not only with the *Death* of our SAVIOUR in this world, but even *"much more"* with His present *Life* in Heaven. We are too much accustomed to think only of the Benefits procured for us by *the Death* of our LORD; and greatly to overlook those Benefits which are procured for us by the present Life of our SAVIOUR. We confine our attention too much to what our LORD did and suffered for us here below, in the days of His weakness and humiliation; and we forget to consider what He is now doing for us, in His power and His glory, at the right hand of the FATHER. So much so indeed, that some seem to think that our SAVIOUR's work for our salvation consisted only in coming down from Heaven *to suffer Death* for us. The words before us, Brethren, should certainly serve to correct this common fault. For S. Paul does not hesitate to use the words " *much more.*" As if he would say, Whatever benefits were procured for us *by the Death of the Son of God* in this world, yet, much more, does our final salvation depend *upon the present Life of our Lord*; that is, on His Life in the presence of the FATHER.

Redemption from the curse of our fallen state and Reconciliation with GOD, was, indeed, the first thing needed for our salvation. This was obtained for us by the Atonement which was made by the Sacrifice of the Death of the LORD. For, even *when we were enemies,* CHRIST died for us, and redeemed us from the curse, and delivered us from the power of Satan, and restored us to the grace of GOD and to the blessed hope of everlasting Life. But the first gift of Justification and Redemption and Reconciliation with GOD is not the same thing as our final salvation. The *beginning* of any work is not the *whole* of it; the foundation of a building is not the superstructure. The redemption of the Israelites out of Egypt was not the *whole* of their salvation, it was not *all* that GOD did for them; it was not the same thing as their entrance into Canaan. The first gift of redemption from the curse and reconciliation with GOD is not *all* that is needful for our final salvation. *Pardon of sin* is not the only thing we need. Pardon of sin is not the same thing as the gift of the power of eternal Life. Reconciliation with GOD is not the same gift as the communication to us and the preservation within us of the power of an endless Life. Deliverance from Hell is not the same thing as exaltation into Heaven. In considering the amazing greatness and the infinite strength of the foundation, we should not, surely, overlook the loftiness and the glory of the superstructure. When a workman has laid the foundation of a building, he has not finished it. The Incarnation of the Eternal SON of GOD; His lowly Nativity here below; His Life of poverty and human weakness here upon earth; His Death upon the Cross, in sorrow, pain, and agony unspeakable; His Resurrection from the dead; *all* this would have been *fruitless* without the Ascension and the present Life in glory at the right hand of the FATHER. The deep roots of a tree, its stem, its branches, its leaves and blossoms; *all* is imperfect, *without the fruit.*

The present Life of the LORD JESUS, in the presence of the FATHER, *this* is the fruit of all that went before, *this* it is which is the means of carrying on and bringing to perfection all that our SAVIOUR began upon earth. He only laid the deep foundation of His great work for our salvation, in His Life and Death here below; He did not *finish* His work then; He only *began* it. He finished, indeed, the Life of suffering; He finished the Sacrifice of Himself in Blood and Death; He finished the work which the FATHER had given Him to do upon earth; but He did not finish His *whole* work for us; He only began it; He only laid the foundation of it in His Life and Death on earth. Now He ever lives to carry on His great work for us in Heaven itself, in power and in glory infinite. Our final salvation depends in some very great and most essential respects, on this present work of our SAVIOUR for us. For S. Paul says, *"Much more shall we be saved by His Life."* Because as He once *died for us,* so now He ever *lives for us.* And, therefore, *apart from this present life for us*, our LORD's Death would not have saved us.

When the LORD JESUS had finished His work on earth, He ascended into Heaven, and appeared in our nature, *the same Lord Jesus*, in the Presence of the FATHER. Then, as it had been clearly prophesied, He received of the FATHER new gifts, and these new gifts were for us and for our salvation: they were therefore gifts necessary for our salvation.

For instance: our LORD then began to be our New Divine Head. The Church began to be the Body of CHRIST, which it never had been before. And it is the object of a Head to give life to all its members. Eternal life must not only be purchased *for us*, but as well actually communicated *to us*, as an indwelling power. The Incarnate LORD therefore is now to us the true Vine, He is the living and the life-giving stem, we the branches; one life circulating through all. By His death He purchased the gift for us, by His life He communicates the gift to us. This is necessary for our salvation. There is now no revealed way of salvation for us, except we be made members of the Body of the Second Adam. "*Much more*" therefore are we now saved "*by His Life.*"

Another instance we may take of the truth

before us. On His Ascension as Man into the Presence of the FATHER, the LORD JESUS entered into His office as a Priest in the true Sanctuary above. Then He began to execute His priestly office in all power and glory before the very Presence of the FATHER. Then He entered in, our true Priest, within the vail, even into Heaven itself, carrying in with Him the Blood of the Sacrifice which had been slain in this outer world, to present or offer that Sacrifice on the heavenly Altar, even on the Mercy-Seat of GOD, before the very Presence of the FATHER; perfectly fulfilling the ancient type, sprinkling the Mercy-Seat of GOD with the all-atoning Blood.

By His Death then in this outer world our LORD *made* the One Sacrifice for sin. By His Life above, He presents that One Sacrifice unceasingly within the vail before the true Mercy-Seat of GOD. It is one thing to make the Sacrifice by His Death; it is another thing to offer or present that Sacrifice before the very Presence of the FATHER at the very heavenly Altar above. If therefore we are saved by His Death, much more shall we be saved by His Life, because He is now living as our Priest before the FATHER.

If then we regard only *these two Offices*, which our LORD is now ever discharging for us, as *our Life-giving Head,* and *our ever ministering Priest,* we may easily understand S. Paul's words, "*much more shall we be saved by His Life.*"

Our final salvation is continually and essentially depending upon this our LORD's present work for us. As *our new Divine Head,* He is our Life, for He is communicating of His own Life to us His members. As *our great High Priest,* He ever lives to make intercession for us, ever taking away our sins through His all-atoning Sacrifice. His *Death* in this world, apart from this His present *Headship,* or apart from this His present *Priesthood,* would not have saved us.

Let none of us then ever suppose that all that our SAVIOUR had to do for our salvation was to come down from Heaven to suffer *death* for us. It is to be feared that it would make but little difference, in the thoughts of *some* concerning our SAVIOUR, if He had never risen from the dead *as Man, in a human body;* or if on His Ascension, He had quite laid aside the human nature; if our SAVIOUR were now in Heaven as GOD only, and not Man also; if His only work for us had been to suffer and *to die for us* in this world. This is to regard the strength of the foundation, and then to disregard the splendour of the lofty superstructure.

We should rather understand that however great are the benefits procured by the Death of CHRIST, yet *much more* great are the benefits procured for us by His Life; however great the foundation, still greater is the building built thereupon. For our LORD only *began* His work for our salvation in His Life and Death here below; now He ever lives, in the power and the glory of the FATHER, *to carry it on*, and *to bring it to a most amazing and glorious issue*.

"*It is* [indeed] *Christ Who died;* yea, rather, (continues the Apostle,) *that is risen again, Who is even at the right hand of God.*"

SERMON VIII.

OUR LORD MADE THE HEAD OF THE CHURCH.

EPH. I. 22.

"AND GAVE HIM TO BE THE HEAD OVER ALL THINGS TO THE CHURCH."

HERE is revealed to us, brethren, one of the infinitely great truths of our Christian faith, viz., that on the Ascension of our LORD into heaven, GOD the FATHER gave Him to be "the Head over all things to the Church."

This doctrine we must receive, of course, simply through faith. Like all the other great articles of the Christian religion, this is entirely above and beyond our mere natural reason; it must be received by faith in Divine Revelation.

On the Ascension of our LORD in our human nature into the highest heaven, GOD the FATHER gave Him to be "the Head over all things to the Church."

Let us then, brethren, now consider this part

of the exceeding great mystery of the Ascension.

I. To understand it rightly, we must first of all bear in mind when our SAVIOUR ascended into heaven, He ascended *in our Human Nature*. In His Divine Nature, being of one substance with the FATHER, He was, and is, always in heaven. In His Divine Nature He had always all power, dominion, and glory. But on the Ascension, He entered into heaven in our human nature. He ascended into heaven, *so* as He had never been there before. He ascended into heaven, no longer simply as GOD, but as "GOD *made Man.*" He entered into heaven, and passed through all the orders and ranks of the heavenly hosts, and went up above all the thrones and dominions, powers, and principalities of heaven, in exceeding great triumph, even until He came to the very throne of the FATHER, where, in our human nature He sat down at the right hand of the Majesty on high. Then the glorious Mystery of the Incarnation was fulfilled in the kingdom of heaven; for then GOD the SON, made Man, was manifest to all the company of heaven, most high in the glory of the FATHER. Thus, then, our LORD ascending in our nature, entering into heaven above, as *Man*, GOD the FATHER most highly exalts Him, and sets Him in our nature at His own right hand, far above all the powers of heaven, and gives Him to be "the Head over all things to the Church."

The same LORD JESUS, Who was once laid in the manger at Bethlehem, and hung on the Cross at Calvary: Who lived on this earth in so great humiliation and abasement, even *He* is now exalted to the right hand of GOD the FATHER, and constituted "the Head over all things to the Church." In His Divine Nature He was one with the FATHER, and had already all power over all the Universe; but now ascending in the Human Nature, He is constituted the Head over all things, for a *new* purpose, for a *special* end, namely, *to the Church*. As GOD He rules over *all the Creation* for ever. But now *as God made Man*, He is given to be the Head over all things "to the Church," which is a New Creation.

II. This, then, brethren, is one of the infinite gifts which the Eternal SON Incarnate obtained of the FATHER on His triumphant Ascension into heaven.

Let us now consider *what this implies;* what is meant by this title, "the Head of the Church?" Now the office of a Head is threefold; it is to *rule over,* to *unite together,* and to *give life*. Let us consider how in all these three respects our ascended and glorified LORD is "the Head of the Church."

1. First; on the Ascension, our LORD is exalted to supreme *Power and Dominion*, to rule as a King over His kingdom. Just as He is ascending from Mount Olivet He says, "All power is given unto Me in heaven and in earth." For He ascends to receive for Himself *a kingdom;* He, the Messiah, ascends to the throne of His glory; He enters into His Regal and Kingly office; He is crowned with all glory and honour in exceeding great triumph; He is seated on the very throne of the FATHER, the throne of the Universe.

In this, brethren, many an ancient type was fulfilled. Then, *the true Joseph*, once hated by his brethren, sold by them, cast into prison, banished from his father's presence, in great affliction and humiliation, is lifted up, exalted to the throne of the kingdom, made ruler over all the land. Then, the true *David*, for many years living in great obscurity and affliction, after much warfare and suffering, gained at last actual possession of his promised kingdom, and seated himself in the true Jerusalem, and was enthroned in all glory. Then, the true *Ark*, which for a long period had wandered in the wilderness, and had been captured by the Philistines, and had sojourned in houses and in tabernacles, was carried up to Jerusalem with exceeding great joy of all the tribes of Israel,

David himself leading the procession, dancing before the ark with all his might, and then distributing gifts to all the people. In like manner, our LORD and SAVIOUR Himself, after a life of the greatest suffering and abasement here below, was carried up with exceeding great glory and triumph of all the heavenly host, into the very Presence of GOD, and entered into His resting place, obtaining new gifts of grace for men. Thus, then, in this sense, the ascended and glorified LORD is *Head* over all things to the Church; He sits on the throne of His glory to *rule as a king* over all things, *and that for the Church.*

2. Next; the office of a Head is *to unite together.* The word *Head* implies not only *power and dominion* but also *union—union in one body;* for if there is *a Head,* there must needs be also *a Body.* This is therefore another great Article of the Christian Faith: as S. Paul declares, in Ephesians iv., where he briefly sums up seven of the main Articles of Christian Unity, beginning with this: "There is One Body"—one mystical Body, of which CHRIST Himself is the *Divine Head, and we the members.*

As it is also in the verse before us, "And gave Him to be the Head over all things to the Church, which is His Body." This is one of the great and fundamental Articles of the Christian Faith, "There is one Body;" the Body, of which CHRIST Himself is the Head. This mystical Body *began to be* on the Ascension of our LORD and the coming of the HOLY GHOST. On the day of Pentecost it began on earth; then men *began to be made members of the Body of* CHRIST. Then the kingdom of heaven, the kingdom of the Regeneration, began on earth.

This was the very end and object of the Incarnation of the Eternal SON of GOD, that He might thus become the Beginning of a new Creation—that He might thus become to us a New Adam—that He might be made "the True Vine," into which we might be engrafted, so that there might be constituted "a new Body," a new Creation, His mystical Body, the fulness of Him Who now filleth all in all. There is therefore, now "one Body," the Body of CHRIST, of which He is the Head; all the members of which are united into one Body through their union with Him Who is the Head of the Body. For it is *union with the Head* which unites all into one, all the members into one body.

This union, brethren, with our Divine Head is, of course, not a mere figure of speech; it does not mean a mere union of sentiment or of judgment or of will, but as the union of the branches with the stem of the vine is a *real* union; or, as the union of the various members of our natural body with the head is a real union;

even so, our union with the Divine Head of this mystical Body, is a *real* and *true* union, although beyond and above the reach of our knowledge.

Now, therefore, the Eternal SON of GOD Incarnate is constituted *the Head* of the Body. In this respect *He unites* all into one body. This is another office of the Head.

3. Thirdly, the office of a Head is also to *give life*. As it is in the kingdom of nature, so it is also in the kingdom of grace: without union with the *head*, none of our natural members can live; union with the head is quite essential to life. So it is in the body mystical. Or, in the *vine:* none of the branches can live, and grow, and bring forth fruit, except through union with the stem; life flows into them through their union with the stem. So it is also with the Body of CHRIST.

None of us have *any eternal life* abiding in us, except through our union with our Divine Head. Our Salvation, our very Life, comes to us, entirely and only, in the most essential sense of all, through our membership in the Body of CHRIST, through our union with our Divine Head.

Thus, then, brethren, as the office of a *head* is threefold,—namely, to have power and dominion to *rule* over the members, and also to *unite* all the members into one body, and also to *give life* to all the members,—so we believe concerning *Him* Who is *the Head over all things to the Church*. On His triumphant Ascension into glory, GOD the SON, made for ever Man, was constituted the Head of His mystical Body, the Church; so that, by virtue of that office, He *rules* as a King; He *unites* us into one mystical Body; He *gives life* to each member of that Body.

Here, if time permitted, we might consider *the special means of union* with our Divine Head —namely, *the two Sacraments*, appointed by our LORD Himself for that end; for in the first Sacrament we are first of all made *members of Christ*, and in the second Sacrament our union with CHRIST is continually *sustained and preserved*. These are the divinely-appointed means or instruments in or by which, through the mighty working of the HOLY GHOST, our membership in the mystical Body of CHRIST is conveyed to us, and preserved. This it is, brethren, which makes the Holy Sacraments so *necessary to our salvation;* because in one of them our union with our Divine Head is begun, and in the other it is preserved.

But let me now conclude with one or two *practical uses* of the doctrine of the text.

1. Consider first, brethren, *the infinite dignity* of your membership in the Body of CHRIST.

Consider the unspeakable honour and glory of this gift that is given you, one of the fruits of the Ascension,—that you should be made a member of that mystical Body of which the LORD GOD Incarnate Himself is the Head. *There is one Body*, of which the ascended and glorified LORD is the Head, and you the members. We are united in one Body with Him Who is exalted most highly in our nature,—even on the Throne of the FATHER.

For let us bear in mind that this gift is granted us *individually*,—not merely to the Church at large, but to *each one individually;* just as S. Paul said to the Corinthians, "Now ye are the Body of CHRIST, and members in particular;" that is, members *individually, one by one.*

To every one of us, therefore, is this gift granted; to every one who is baptized has this gift been given, viz., to be a member of the Body of CHRIST,—a member of that mystical Body, of which GOD the SON Incarnate is the Head. Just as S. Paul had no hesitation in saying to *all* the Corinthian Christians that they were members of the Body of CHRIST, *one by one*, although amongst them were many sinful and evil members; even so must it be said still: the gift of membership is granted to us *all*,—even this great gift of honour and dignity, to be *members of Christ*. He, our ascended LORD, gives Himself in our Baptism to be a new, Divine, Life-giving Head, to each one of us.

This infinite gift of union with our Divine Head, brethren, confers upon us exceeding great honour and dignity indeed. By virtue of our *first* creation in Adam, our place amongst the creatures of GOD was high and glorious; but how much more so by virtue of *this* our new creation in CHRIST, *this* our union with *Him* Who reigns above in glory on the Throne of GOD.

But with every gift of GOD comes not only honour and dignity, but also *duty and responsibility*.

2. Let us therefore consider, in the next place, the *exceeding great responsibility of this*. Even of all His good gifts in *nature* which GOD is continually granting us, He will require an account. Even *these* GOD gives us for certain purposes. Even our natural life in Adam is a great gift, bringing with it to every one great duties and responsibilities. How much *higher* duties and *heavier* responsibilities are laid upon us, as members of the Second Adam! for here are the richest and the best gifts of GOD, His gifts of grace in the kingdom of CHRIST.

But of these responsibilities, brethren, and of the rule of GOD's final judgment, we are very forgetful. Too generally we misuse and pervert all God's good gifts : both natural gifts and spiritual gifts are too generally all wasted away and lost by us ; and so, in the end, many a branch in the True Vine will be broken off, and cast into the fire, for lack of fruit ; many a barren member of the Body of Christ will be cast out of His kingdom, in the great trying day.

Oh, consider, therefore, brethren, how you are using your gifts in the kingdom of Christ. You have been made a member of the mystical Body of Christ; but, *for what end?* That you might be dead indeed unto sin, but alive unto God. You have been created anew in Christ Jesus; but, *for what end?* That you might bring forth the fruit of good works, Christian good works; that you might live unto Him Who died for you, Who now lives for you.

Are these ends, then, being fulfilled in you? Are you walking as becometh saints, members of that Body of which the Lord Himself is the Head ; preparing with all earnestness and diligence for His Second Coming to judge the world, that then you may be found in peace, and be accounted worthy to ascend into glory?

3. For, lastly, consider, brethren, *that complete restoration*, that perfect deliverance from evil, that most amazing exaltation to glory and

joy unspeakable, which must follow from our union with our Divine Head. If that union be not dissolved by sin,—if we abide in CHRIST,—to what exceeding heights of glory must it raise us in the end! even to be with Him where He is, to behold His glory, to see His unveiled Face, to ascend *ourselves* also into the glories of His eternal kingdom, and so to be for ever *with the Lord;* ourselves made like unto Him in His everlasting and glorious kingdom; to reign with Him in glory; to serve Him continually with all the restored perfections of our nature.

Then will come the Second Ascension, when the LORD GOD Incarnate will ascend in glory and triumph; not then *alone,* but with all the company of the elect. Then His Mystical Body, the Church, purified and perfected, every evil member broken off, made all pure, and spotless, and glorious, will be presented faultless before the Presence of His glory with exceeding joy. For our SAVIOUR and Redeemer has said, "In My FATHER's house are many mansions: if it were not so, I would have told you. I go to prepare a place for you. And if I go and prepare a place for you, I will come again, and receive you unto Myself, that where I am, there ye may be also."

SERMON IX.

THE EXTENSION OF OUR LORD'S PRESENCE.

EPH. IV. 10.

"HE THAT DESCENDED IS THE SAME ALSO THAT ASCENDED UP, FAR ABOVE ALL HEAVENS, THAT HE MIGHT FILL ALL THINGS."

These words of Divine Revelation declare plainly one of the infinitely great consequences of the Ascension of the LORD JESUS. The Ascension of the Incarnate Word into the Glory of the FATHER could not but be fruitful in many Gifts to Man. This is one of them; He ascended in order "*that He might fill all things.*" This article of the Christian revelation deserves our deepest consideration.

To our natural senses and to our human reason it might seem that the Ascension of our LORD would be to us the loss of His Presence. We might have thought that by His Ascension all things would have been emptied of His

Presence, so that we could now only mourn for His absence; thinking of Him only as absent, not present. But quite on the contrary: "*He ascended, that He might fill all things*" with His Presence.

Here we must distinguish between the Presence of our LORD as GOD only, and His Presence as GOD Incarnate. Before our LORD was made Man, He was present, as GOD, everywhere; as GOD, being of one substance with the FATHER, He then, as still, filled all things with His Presence. But when He was made Man, He was present, before His Ascension, as Man, only in one place at a time. In His earthly body, the LORD JESUS was subject to the laws of an earthly body; He was not present everywhere at the same time; His Presence was partial and local and external. But now, since He ascended and has been glorified, the same LORD JESUS is able to fill all things with His Presence; He ascended in the human nature in order to this very end, that in the human nature He might be able to fill all things. For at His Resurrection His natural Body was made a spiritual Body; and at His Ascension that spiritual Body was glorified, being lifted up into the very glory and power of the FATHER. So that the powers and capacities of this ascended glorified spiritual Body of the LORD JESUS are now beyond and above all our present knowledge, raised above the laws of a mere earthly body.

Now, therefore, we can believe that the same LORD JESUS is able to be present throughout the whole Church at the same time. Now our LORD is able to fill all things, not as GOD only, as He did before His Incarnation, but as Man also. Now He is able to be present both in His Manhood and in His Godhead, wheresoever He pleases. Now the Manhood and the Godhead are for ever in Him indivisibly united; so that He fills all things, not only as GOD, but as GOD Incarnate. This is revealed to us as one consequence of the Ascension of the LORD JESUS into Glory.

Notwithstanding, we learn from the first chapter of this Epistle, that this Presence of our LORD is in some way limited or restricted. This filling of all things with the Presence of the Incarnate Word is restricted, in some special manner, to the Church, which is the Body of CHRIST. For it is there written, that on our LORD'S Ascension GOD the FATHER "*gave Him to be the Head over all things to the Church, which is His Body, the Fulness of Him Who now filleth all in all.*"

By calling the Church by this title, "*the Fulness of Christ,*" S. Paul teaches us that our

LORD now fills all things, in some special manner, in the Church, which is His mystical Body.

We learn, therefore, that as the spirit of a man fills, quickens, and sustains his whole natural body; even so, in some like manner, the Presence of the LORD fills His whole mystical Body by the Spirit. This Presence is the Presence, we must bear in mind, both of the Manhood and of the Godhead which are in CHRIST JESUS our LORD.

We may now consider *three* special ways in which it is revealed that this benefit is now communicated unto us. For all the benefits of the Ascension are for our participation, for our life, for our salvation, for our endless glory.

We may perceive then the present truth, how our ascended and glorified LORD JESUS now fills all things for the Church which is His mystical Body, when we call to mind His promise, "*Where two or three are gathered together in My Name there am I in the midst.*" Before the Ascension, we never read of the LORD JESUS being in the midst of His disciples in more than one place at a time. His Presence was locally restricted by the laws of an earthly body. But now, since He ascended into power and glory, He is able to be present in the midst in ten thousand assemblies at the same moment; even the same LORD JESUS, perfect Man as well as perfect GOD. Before the Ascension, speaking to Nicodemus the LORD spoke of Himself as "*the Son of Man, Who is in Heaven.*" Even then He was not so present upon earth as Man as to be absent as GOD from Heaven. And now He is not so present in Heaven as to be absent from us here below, both as Man and as GOD. The promise of His special Presence is fulfilled whenever two or three are gathered together in His Name.

Next let us consider that our LORD now gives Himself to each individual member of His Church in the capacity of an indwelling life-giving Head. His Presence is now granted to us and communicated to us so as to be within us, as our life, our strength, our joy, our glory. As our LORD said, "*I in them;*" and as S. Paul writes, "*Know ye not your own selves, how that Jesus Christ is in you, except ye be reprobates?*" This union with CHRIST, this membership with our Divine Head, the LORD Incarnate, the Second Adam; this indwelling of CHRIST as a quickening Spirit, this, we may well say, is our very present salvation. His Presence is not now merely external, as before the Ascension; but it is given to be within us. He is our indwelling and life-giving Head.

And then also, thirdly, the Presence of the

LORD Incarnate now fills all things in the Church, we are plainly taught, by the Holy Communion of His Body and of His Blood. He Himself makes good His own word: "*This is My Body, this is My Blood,*" at every celebration of the Holy Eucharist. Those words are no mere figurative expressions, but most real and true. When our LORD speaks with His dying breath, not in any parable, but at the institution of that positive ordinance which is the one distinguishing rite of worship for the whole of the Christian Dispensation, and says, "*This is My Body,*" who shall venture so to interpret His meaning as to make those words mean, "*This is not My Body?*" In a most real sense, then, although in a profound mystery transcending our knowledge, at ten thousand altars at the same moment our LORD makes good His own great saying, "*This is My Body.*" At ten thousand altars at the same time this mystery is fulfilled; His Body is present, really and substantially, "*verily and indeed,*" not in any mere figure of speech. And this special Presence of the Body of CHRIST in this holy Sacrament is granted *for our participation.* The command is, "*Take, eat, this is My Body.*" And S. Paul writes to the same effect: "*The Bread which we break, is it not the Communion of the Body of Christ?*"

Here, therefore, we are individually made partakers of the Body of CHRIST. For here the Bread which we break is no mere figure of something absent; but it is a sign, Divinely given, of something present; and that Presence is granted *for our participation*. And then our LORD Himself instructs us as to the effect of this Holy Communion of His most precious Body and Blood, for He says, "*Whoso eateth My Flesh and drinketh My Blood, dwelleth in Me, and I in him.*"

By this special means, therefore, the Incarnate Word comes to dwell within us, giving Himself to us. By this most holy Communion of His Body and Blood He communicates His Presence to us individually, from time to time, to be within us. So our union with Him Who is our Life is nourished and preserved, and we are made already partakers of His Nature. The seed or germ of that restored Manhood which is in Him, our indwelling Head, is planted in us, to be developed at the Resurrection into the glories of eternity.

By these considerations we can understand, in some measure, that new name and title of the Church, which has been given it since the Ascension of GOD Incarnate, namely, "*The Body of Christ*," or "*The Fulness of Him Who now filleth all in all.*" For the LORD Incarnate ascended in order "*that He might fill all things.*"

Now, therefore, our spiritual condition is far above that of any of the saints of the elder dispensations: for now the LORD's Presence is not only with us, but in us; to guide, to sanctify, to comfort, and to save, every willing, believing, obedient soul.

Now is fulfilled the prophetic promise, "*I will dwell in them and walk in them;*" so that S. Paul exhorts us to all pureness of living by this very motive: "*Know ye not that your bodies are the members of Christ?*"

SERMON X.

THE NEW CONSTITUTION OF THE CHURCH.

Col. i. 18.

"AND HE IS THE HEAD OF THE BODY, THE CHURCH."

The Prophet Isaiah foretold the greater glory of the Church which should be revealed at the Advent of the Messiah, when he prophesied, "*Thou shalt be called by a new name, which the mouth of the Lord shall name.*" (Isa. lxii. 2.)

For it was meet that when the Eternal SON of GOD Himself was manifested in the flesh and received His new name, *Jesus*, the Church should also be called by a new name. This new name corresponds to the new constitution which the Church has now received, since the Incarnation of the SON of GOD and His Ascension into glory. S. Paul alone has revealed unto us this new name; it is, "*The Body of Christ.*"

The Church is now what it never was before, the Mystical Body of CHRIST. For the Incarnation of the SON of GOD has changed all things to us, and made all things new to us. S. Paul often speaks of the Church as being a new creation. For instance, in 2 Cor. v. 17, "*If any man be in Christ, he is a new creation,*" for so is the original word. And in Eph. ii. 10, "*We are created in Christ Jesus.*" For by Adam we enter into the natural creation, but by CHRIST we enter into the new creation, which is His Body.

And in the passage before us, it is remarkable that S. Paul introduces the Church as a new creation. For having spoken of the Eternal SON of GOD as the Creator of all the powers and creations of GOD, whether in heaven or in earth, he proceeds to speak of Him as "*The Head of the Body, the Church.*"

This is the new creation, the Mystical Body of the SON of GOD, dependent on His Incarnation. For He was given to be the Head of the Church when He ascended in the human nature into the Presence of the FATHER. Then the Church began to be "*the Body of Christ, the Fulness of Him Who now filleth all in all.*" (Eph. i. 23.)

So that now as soon as any one is baptized into CHRIST, he is a new creation. As soon as any one is made a member of CHRIST, he is united to a new Divine Head, the Incarnate Word, the Second Adam. As soon as any one is born again of Water and the HOLY GHOST, he enters into the new kingdom of GOD Incarnate.

This is our regeneration; this is a gift of the power and grace of GOD which never was and never could have been granted to any of the Saints of the older dispensations. It could not have been said to them, as it is now said to us, *" Now ye are the Body of Christ, and members in particular."* (1 Cor. xii. 27.)

Thus then the Church is now constituted in CHRIST, the Second Adam. It is a Mystical Body, of which the Incarnate SON of GOD is Himself the Head, and we who are baptized the members.

All this, we must understand, is no mere figure of speech, it is no mere high sounding metaphor, but it is a most real and glorious truth, although there is in it a profound Mystery, reaching far above and beyond our knowledge. The union of the members with the Head is *mystical*, that is, we do not pretend to say or explain *how it is*. It is one of the deep mysteries of our Christian Faith, that *" there is One Body,"* a new mystical Body, deriving its existence and its life from the Ascended Incarnate LORD. It is, strictly speaking, a Divine organization, a heavenly communion, a mystical fellowship. It is the extension of the Incarnation.

The Church could not be this Body of CHRIST until the CHRIST Himself was constituted. The mystical Body of the SON of GOD could not, of course, begin to be, until the SON of GOD had Himself been made Man, and as Man had ascended into heaven and been glorified. But on that consummation of the great Mystery of the Incarnation, the Church began to be "*the Body of Christ.*" It is now the extension of the Incarnation, a new Divine Communion, a Living Organization, even the Mystical Body of the Second Adam, the Incarnate Word. For the SON of GOD was made the Second Adam, not that He should remain alone in His Manhood, but that He should be a new source and head of life to the fallen family of the first Adam. He was made the Second Adam in order that He might unite us as members to Himself; in order that He might be to us the True Vine, and that we might be grafted into Him, and so receive of the life which is in Him. He was made the New Man, in order that we, being made members of Him, might receive life of His life, and so become possessors of that restored manhood which is in Him our Divine Head.

Accordingly on the Day of Pentecost, the first day of the new dispensation, the dispensation of the HOLY GHOST, men here below began to be joined on to the LORD Incarnate. And in the same Sacrament of Baptism we receive this same distinguishing gift of the new dispensation of grace purchased for all mankind by our great Redeemer; we are made members of CHRIST, the Second Adam, the Incarnate SON of GOD now reigning in glory, our New Head.

This is the new constitution of the Church since the Ascension of the LORD JESUS into the glory of the FATHER. This is our new and better gift of membership with the Second Adam. This is our new birth, our regeneration, our exceeding great glory, that we are members of a Mystical Body of which the Incarnate SON of GOD is the Life-giving Head.

This is the very order of our great salvation, that we may thus receive life of His Life; and so, if we duly cherish this gift of grace, receive a participation of that restored Manhood which is in Him, our Divine Head, and so be lifted up for ever, at the Resurrection, into the glories of His Presence.

SERMON XI.

THE ONE BODY OF CHRIST.

EPH. IV. 4.

"THERE IS ONE BODY."

SINCE the Ascension of the SON of GOD, next to the Doctrine of the *Holy Trinity,* there now comes this Doctrine; *" There is one Body."* This is the order in which it comes in the Apostles' Creed. For when we have professed our belief in *Three* several *Persons* of the *One Godhead,* then next we say; *"I believe in the Holy Catholic Church."* For this is the same Article of Christian faith as that taught us in the Text, *" There is One Body."*

It is however to be feared that many persons in our day repeat this Article of the Creed without at all understanding what it means. What *do* we all mean, brethren, when we solemnly and publicly say, here, before GOD; *"I believe in the Holy Catholic Church ?"*

Let us mark the order in the chapter before us:—S. Paul here sums up the Articles of Christian unity in these seven chief and essential particulars; one *Body*; one *Spirit*; one *Hope*; one *Lord*; one *Faith*; one *Baptism*; one *God and Father of all*. The Article which he places in the very forefront of all, is this; "*There is one Body.*" There can be then no real Christian unity *without this*. We may indulge in lofty imaginations, and in high-sounding words, about *unity*; but true and real Christian unity depends in the first place upon this Article; "*There is one Body.*"

We cannot therefore understand rightly, *what Christian unity is*, unless we have an intelligent faith in this Article of the Creed, "*I believe in the Holy Catholic Church.*"

1. First of all, it may be well to consider *what the Holy Catholic Church is not*. It does not mean a Company formed by all *good* and *sincere* Christians. This is quite a mistaken notion. Because, such good and sincere Christians do not form any Body or Church, by themselves. *God* knows them, one by one, but *God only*. They are not formed into any one Body; they do not constitute any Church, by themselves, as yet.

After the Judgment day, they *will* be alone; then they will be one holy and perfected Body;

all pure and glorious. Then all evil will be cast out of His kingdom, by our LORD Himself; but not till then. At present (He expressly teaches us,) both tares and wheat grow together in the same field: the good members and the evil members of His Church are mixed together. It is, therefore, quite a mistaken idea, to think of the *Holy Catholic Church of Christ*, as consisting of only all the *good* and the *sincere amongst Christians*.

2. Next; the *Holy Catholic Church* is *not* any mere *human Association*. It is no *self-formed* Institution; it is no mere *worldly* Brotherhood. It is no *human sect*, or religious Society, formed by this or that man, a few years ago. You or I, brethren, have no power, no spiritual authority whatever, to constitute the Church of CHRIST, or any branch of it. It is wholly beyond and above the powers of any mere *man*, to make a Church. This, indeed, is one of the most astonishing acts of presumption of our times; that many people fancy that they have power to *set up a new Church*. They might just as well try to write a *new Bible;* or make a *new Sacrament.* The *Holy Catholic Church* of CHRIST is *not*, then, any human Institution; it is no human sect; no self-formed Society.

3. Once more; it is not any *mere State*

Establishment. No temporal State has any power to make *a Church*, any more than any private individual. A State may, indeed, if it pleases, grant certain privileges, and certain endowments, and certain worldly dignities, to the Holy Catholic Church, which it finds within its territory; and then that branch of the Catholic Church may be called the "*established*" Church of that country: but *that* is a mere *accident; that* does not at all *make* the Church. Neither, if the State takes away those temporal privileges, does *that unmake* the Church. The Church is, in all its essential spiritual nature, independent of the State. It remains perfectly the same, whether the State *establishes* it, or *persecutes* it.

Having thus considered these truths; that the Holy Catholic Church is *not* the collection of all *good* and *sincere* Christians only; that it is *not a human Institution*, nor any *self-made Society;* and that it is *not* any mere *State-Establishment:* let us now endeavour to consider *what it essentially is.*

We must begin at the beginning. GOD the SON was made Man. The Eternal Word was manifest in the flesh. He chose out of His Disciples *twelve* men to be His *Apostles.* These Apostles our LORD sent forth into all nations, with special spiritual power and authority derived from His own Power; for He said to them, just as He was ascending to His throne, "*All power is given unto Me in heaven and in earth, go ye therefore;*" "*as My Father hath sent Me, even so send I you.*" He then commanded them to do *two* things—to *preach* the Gospel to every creature, and then to *baptize;* not only to *preach*, but as well to *baptize*.

Now what was the necessary consequence?

Let us take the case of the great heathen city, Corinth. The Apostles went there, and they *preached the Gospel of the kingdom of Christ.* Some of the Corinthians *believed* what they heard, and then the Apostles *baptized* them. Thus a *new visible society* was at once instituted; a *new brotherhood* was made, and *that* by Divine Authority.

In that city of Corinth, the greater number of the inhabitants remained heathen, but some became Christians. Those who were Christians were formed into one body by their baptism. Their baptism visibly marked them off at once from all the rest of the Corinthians who were not baptized. For baptism has a visible part, as well as an invisible part. At Corinth then there was thus formed a new brotherhood, there was thus formed a new body.

We must consider that this body of the baptized at Corinth was one *visible* body; it was *visibly marked off* from all the other Corinthians by the Sacrament of Baptism.

But let us not look on the *outside* only. That Sacrament of Baptism ordained by CHRIST Himself, has an *inward spiritual part*, as well as an *outward visible part*.

In that holy Sacrament man is born again of water and the HOLY GHOST, and made a member of the Second Adam. The essential gift of Christian Baptism is the gift of membership with CHRIST, the Incarnate LORD, the Second Adam. For now there exists *One Body* of which CHRIST Himself is the *Divine Head*, and of which we who are baptized are the *members*. Just as S. Paul wrote to those very Corinthian Christians, " *Now ye are the Body of Christ, and members one by one.*"

Wherever therefore the Apostles of CHRIST went, they thus set up a new brotherhood, they baptized men everywhere into the Church of CHRIST, they set up the new kingdom of CHRIST in the world. In *Corinth* there was one Church thus instituted; in *Rome* there was one Church thus instituted; in *Ephesus* there was one Church thus instituted, and so on. And all these several Churches in these several places formed but one Church, for they were all united together under the Apostles and under the Ministers whom the Apostles set over them in the LORD; all united in one Holy Eucharist, one *breaking of Bread* on every LORD's Day.

In this manner, brethren, the Holy Catholic Church of CHRIST was set up by the Apostles in all known nations of the world. In this manner the Church was set up here in *England*, if not by S. Paul himself, yet certainly in his lifetime. The unity of the Church was completely provided for before the Apostles left the world. The Church was everywhere set in order under Bishops, Priests, and Deacons. And it continued steadfastly everywhere "*in the Apostles' doctrine and fellowship, and in the breaking of the Bread, and in the prayers.*" This unity of the one Body of CHRIST in the world, this unity of the Holy Catholic Church of CHRIST continued unbroken for the first thousand years.

All branches of the Church in different nations were in communion one with another. *Two* Churches in the *same* place was a thing unheard of, a thing never dreamt of anywhere. The sin of *schism* was understood to *be* a sin, a very *great* and *grievous* sin. The precept, "*Love the brotherhood*," was then understood and acted upon. "*I believe in the Holy Catholic Church,*" was an Article of Faith powerfully influencing the heart and life; binding all

H

Christians in one body throughout the known world.

But now, any little company of people that please to do so, think themselves at liberty to separate themselves, and to constitute a new religious society, and to call it a new Church. In our day also, it is true, that many great and grievous hindrances exist, which prevent us from realizing this fundamental Article of Faith, "*There is One Body,*" the Mystical Body of CHRIST, a Body which has not only an inward spiritual mystical unity, but as well a certain definite outward organization in the world, begun by the Apostles of CHRIST, and continued ever since to our day; in which outward organization, however, we must sadly confess, there are now grievous hindrances to perfect intercommunion and fellowship. Still, in spite of all these present hindrances, we must hold the Article of the Faith all the more firmly, "*There is One Body,*" rejecting every opinion and every practice which is inconsistent with this truth.

For this One Body is the Mystical Body of the Incarnate SON of GOD. In the invisible and mystical unity of this Body we are united as members to our Divine Head. And in its visible unity we ought all to be perfectly joined together, all worshipping one GOD and one

Lord together, with one mouth and one heart.

Against all present difficulties we must believe in the existence of this One Body, we must adhere to it, we must seek its edification, we must receive the Sacraments of Christ in it, and continually should we pray for a restoration of visible unity amongst all its branches.

SERMON XII.

THE NEW KINGDOM OF THE SON OF MAN.

S. MATTH. XVI. 28.

"VERILY I SAY UNTO YOU, THERE BE SOME STANDING HERE, WHICH SHALL NOT TASTE OF DEATH, TILL THEY SEE THE SON OF MAN COMING IN HIS KINGDOM."

IN S. Mark's Gospel, the words are, *"Till they have seen the Kingdom of God come with power."* In S. Luke's Gospel, it is, *"Till they see the Kingdom of God."* The meaning of this saying of our LORD's is for the most part plain enough. Some of the people then standing before Him should not die, till they had seen the Kingdom of GOD actually come with power; or, in the words of S. Matthew, till they had seen our LORD actually coming in His Kingdom. All is plain enough, except the expression, *" coming in His Kingdom."* Our LORD does not say, *" coming to judge the world,"* but "*coming in His Kingdom;*" coming, not in weakness, but "*coming in power.*"

Some commentators explain this as referring to the destruction of Jerusalem, which took place about thirty years after our LORD spoke these words, which doubtless some of those then standing before our LORD lived to witness. Our LORD might certainly be said in some sense to have then come with power to destroy that city; but it seems hardly satisfactory to say that He then came in His Kingdom.

Other commentators explain the saying of our LORD before us, as referring to His Transfiguration. It is true, our LORD then appeared in glory, but it was only for a moment or two. It is hardly satisfactory to say that His Kingdom then came. It seems rather fanciful to say that a King came in His Kingdom with power, when He had yet all His deepest sufferings to endure, all His lowest weakness to undergo, when He was still in His great humiliation, having even the death of the Cross to suffer. A king, rather, comes in his kingdom, in power, to reign, not to suffer at all.

The long promised Kingdom of the Messiah could hardly be said, with any degree of propriety, to have come, or to have actually begun, at His momentary Transfiguration. When, then, did the LORD actually come in

His Kingdom? when did the LORD JESUS come, with power, as a King in His Kingdom, not to suffer any more, but to reign? As soon, indeed, as the LORD from Heaven was born into our human family, it might be properly said, "*The Kingdom of God, the Kingdom of Heaven, is at hand;*" that is, as the Jews all perfectly understood those Titles, the Kingdom which GOD had promised to give the Messiah, the New Kingdom given from Heaven, the Kingdom of the Son of Man, the Kingdom of the Son of David, is at hand.

But when did it actually come? Certainly it came, in this world, on the Great Day of Pentecost, with power of the HOLY GHOST. On the Ascension of the Son of Man into Heaven, this New Kingdom began in Heaven above. For then He was received up into glory, even the LORD JESUS, and sat on the right hand of the Throne of the FATHER: then the Incarnate LORD received all power in Heaven above and on Earth beneath; then He was given to be the Head over all things for the Church which is His Body. Then the LORD JESUS began to reign in glory as King of kings and LORD of lords. Then the New Kingdom of the Son of Man began in Heaven above. And this Kingdom came down to earth and began here below on the day of Pentecost, by the coming of the HOLY GHOST. For by His abiding Presence the Presence of our LORD is restored to us; by His abiding Presence the Incarnate LORD now fills all things in His Church.

On the great day of Pentecost, a day foretold and marked out from ages by a Divinely-ordained Festival, the New Kingdom of the Messiah actually began here upon earth. The Son of Man came, in the power of the HOLY GHOST, in His Kingdom. On that Holy day the Kingdom of Heaven was opened upon earth to all believers. That was the first day of the New Dispensation of the HOLY GHOST. Then men here below began to be joined on to a new Divine Head, being incorporated into the Mystical Body of the Second Adam, by a New Birth of Water and of the HOLY GHOST. Then all things began to be made new. Then men began to be entered into the Kingdom of GOD Incarnate.

On that day of Pentecost the New Jerusalem began to descend out of Heaven, having the glory of GOD in her. For is it not of the very glory of GOD, that we are now made members of the LORD Incarnate? Are we not even now entered into the Kingdom of Heaven, being thus joined on to our new Divine Head reigning on the Throne of His glory! Hereby are we come to this City of the Living GOD, the New Jerusalem, which is built on the twelve Apostolic foundations, *Jesus Christ* Himself being its chief corner-stone. Never should we forget our present position in the Church of CHRIST, which is His Body. Ever should we look upon ourselves as Members of the Second Adam, living in the midst of the Mysteries of the Kingdom of GOD Incarnate.

A blind man, however, may be in the full light of the noonday sun, and yet not know it. The people at Nazareth lived next door to the *Lord Jesus*, and saw Him go in and out amongst them year by year, and yet did not fear or tremble, not knowing Him.

So it may be with us still. For the Kingdom of the CHRIST is for the most part as yet an object only of faith. Only they who are walking by faith can discern its Presence. Only they who are earnestly striving to fulfil the Vows of their Baptism can realise the amazing truth, that they are living in the New Kingdom of Heaven; not indeed in Heaven, but in the Kingdom of Heaven upon earth, which is the porch of the very Heaven of GOD itself.

SERMON XIII.

THE MINISTRY ON EARTH.

S. MATTH. XXVIII. 16—20.

"THEN THE ELEVEN DISCIPLES WENT AWAY UNTO GALILEE, INTO A MOUNTAIN WHERE JESUS HAD APPOINTED THEM. AND WHEN THEY SAW HIM, THEY WORSHIPPED HIM, BUT SOME DOUBTED. AND JESUS CAME, AND SPAKE UNTO THEM, SAYING, ALL POWER IS GIVEN UNTO ME IN HEAVEN AND IN EARTH. GO YE THEREFORE, AND TEACH ALL NATIONS; BAPTIZING THEM IN THE NAME OF THE FATHER, AND OF THE SON, AND OF THE HOLY GHOST; TEACHING THEM TO OBSERVE ALL THINGS WHATSOEVER I HAVE COMMANDED YOU; AND, LO, I AM WITH YOU ALWAY, EVEN UNTO THE END OF THE WORLD. AMEN."

THIS passage of Holy Scripture, brethren, records the final commission given by our LORD JESUS CHRIST to His Apostles—just before His Ascension into Heaven. I need hardly say, therefore, that this is a passage of very special importance. Because it is only *under this commission* from the *Divine Head* of the Church that *any one,* in *any age,* can rightfully minister in the Word and Sacraments of CHRIST. Let me then ask you to mark carefully the several parts of the passage before us.

1. Our LORD makes a special appointment to meet *the eleven disciples,*—not *all* the disciples, but the *eleven* disciples,—that is, *the eleven Apostles,* on a certain mountain in Galilee,— generally supposed to be Mount Tabor. And when they had assembled together there, then our LORD appeared unto them. As soon as they beheld Him, "*they worshipped Him,*" but "*some doubted*" whether it were He or not; for at first it seems that He was at some distance from them. But then, "*Jesus came,*" that is, He came nearer to them, and He spake unto them, so that all doubt was removed from their minds. And He said unto them, "*All Power is given unto Me in Heaven and in earth. Go ye therefore, and teach all nations; baptizing them in the Name of the Father, and of the Son, and of the Holy Ghost; teaching them to observe all things whatsoever I have commanded you; and, lo, I am with you alway, even unto the end of the world. Amen.*"

2. These words, brethren, we should *carefully* mark. *As God,* indeed, our LORD had possessed *all power* from all eternity. This

gift of *all power*, we should understand, was not given to Him in His DIVINE Nature; *nothing* could be *added* to His Power, so far He was one with the FATHER and the HOLY GHOST.

But we must bear in mind that our LORD was just on the point of ascending into Heaven so as He had never been there before; He was now just about to appear in the Presence of the FATHER in *our human* nature; He was just going to enter into Heaven *as Man*. It is to Him *as Man* therefore that this New Gift is given. It is to our LORD ascending *in our nature* that GOD the FATHER gives all *power in Heaven and in earth*. Just as S. Paul reveals to us in Ephesians i.—"*God raised Him from the dead, and set Him at His own right hand in the heavenly places, far above all principality, and power, and might, and dominion, and every name that is named, not only in this world, but also in that which is to come: and hath put all things under His feet, and gave Him to be the Head over all things to the Church, which is His body, the fulness of Him that filleth all in all.*"

On our LORD's Ascension into Heaven, then, as Man, GOD the FATHER thus most highly exalted Him; He gave Him *all power both in Heaven and in earth;* He gave Him a *New Office*, making Him (as S. Paul expresses it) "*Head over all things to the Church."* Being, therefore, just about to ascend, our LORD speaks of this New Power over all things, as *already given* Him; *"All Power is given unto Me in Heaven and in earth. Go ye therefore, and teach all nations; baptizing them in the Name of the Father, and of the Son, and of the Holy Ghost; teaching them to observe all things whatsoever I have commanded you; and, lo, I am with you alway, even unto the end of the world. Amen."*

3. And now, brethren, let us mark what is *the first exercise* which our LORD makes of this His supreme Power, as *Head over all things to the Church.* It is to give power and authority to His eleven Apostles. For the Divine Head of the Church says to them, "GO YE, THEREFORE." We must observe the force of the word *" therefore."* It is as much as to say, *" In consequence of this Power, which is now given unto Me, as Head of the Church, I give you power and commandment to go out for Me into all nations of the world." " As the Father hath sent Me, even so I now send you."* I appoint and authorize you to be My first Apostles; the first ministers of My Grace; the first rulers of My kingdom; the founders of My Church upon earth.

4. Next let us mark *the duties* which our

LORD then laid upon the eleven. They were specially authorized and commanded to teach and *to baptize* in all nations in the name of CHRIST. They were to *teach* all nations *to believe* and *to observe all things whatsoever the Lord had taught and commanded them;* not only to teach them to *believe in Christ*, but as well to believe all *His words*, and to keep all *His sayings*. And they were also *to baptize* all men, in all nations, into the name of the ever-blessed Trinity, the FATHER, the SON, and the HOLY GHOST.

These two things our LORD specially commanded the eleven to do—to *teach*, and to *baptize*—to preach the Gospel of His Grace, to teach the mysteries of His kingdom; and also to baptize men into His Church. *Not only* (you will mark, brethren) to *preach the Gospel of Christ*, but also to *set up the Church of Christ* in all nations; *not only to teach the truth as it is in Jesus*, but also to *baptize men* everywhere into a *New Brotherhood*. For in the Holy Sacrament of Baptism we are all baptized into one Body, all made members of the Church of CHRIST. Whether, then, in Europe, Asia, Africa, or America,—whether Hindoo, New Zealander, Hottentot, Chinese, Englishman, or North American Indian,— whether Jew or Gentile,—*all* are commanded to be taught the mysteries of the Kingdom of CHRIST, and *all* are commanded to be baptized into the Church of CHRIST.

And here let us again mark the fact, that our LORD made this appointment *only with the eleven;* our LORD gave this special power and authority, *not* to *all* the disciples in general, but only to a certain number chosen out of them—only to the eleven. The ordinary disciples therefore could not rightfully *take upon themselves* to teach and to baptize unless they were called and appointed to do so by the Apostles. For GOD is the author of unity and of order—not of division and confusion. CHRIST has built His Church, not in division, but in perfect unity, if indeed we will all observe what He has commanded.

These duties, then, the Apostles of CHRIST proceeded to discharge, as soon as the LORD had ascended, and as soon as He had sent down the HOLY GHOST to give them the power to speak in all the languages of the world, and to strengthen them, and to guide them into all truth. Then they went forth in the Name of CHRIST, and for CHRIST, into all the nations that were then known, as it is recorded in the Acts of the Apostles. Never have there been since any missionaries like them. They went forth, under this Divine commission, and taught and baptized everywhere, the LORD Himself working with them and by them.

And so, by this means, brethren, the Gospel of CHRIST was thus preached, and the Church of CHRIST was thus established, *here in England*, and here it has remained ever since; and *we*, brethren, have been thus baptized into the Church of CHRIST by the LORD's command. Thus the Apostles of CHRIST fulfilled their sacred Ministry, teaching men everywhere to observe all things whatsoever the LORD had taught and commanded them, and setting up throughout the then known world one Holy Catholic Church, baptizing men everywhere into a New Brotherhood—all branches of it being in perfect unity one with another. The Christians at Ephesus, e. g., were all baptized into one Body, all lived together in unity, all obeyed the same spiritual Rulers, all worshipped GOD together in one communion and fellowship, all met every LORD's Day round the same Altar of CHRIST, for the one peculiar and distinguishing Act of Christian worship, the Holy Eucharist. There were not *several* bodies of Christians at *Ephesus*, or *several* bodies of Christians at *Rome*, and so on—all worshipping GOD apart—but only one body, or one Church, in one place; the Church at *Ephesus* being in unity with the Church at

Rome; and so on, in all nations. So that there was *One Holy Catholic Church* thus set up by CHRIST and His Apostles in all nations. So we always confess in our Creed, "*I believe in the Holy Catholic Church,*" thus Divinely set up.

Have *you*, brethren, an intelligent faith in this Article of the Apostles' Creed? Do you believe in this Holy Catholic Church of CHRIST thus set up in all Nations by the Apostles of CHRIST? Or do you, as many do, believe rather in *some modern sect*, set up by this man or that man a few years ago?

One other point in our text, brethren, remains for our consideration. Having given the eleven His final commandment, His final commission, the Divine Head of the Church adds a *very special promise,* "*Lo, I am with you, alway, even unto the end of the world. Amen.*" How then could this promise be understood? because *those Eleven Apostles* soon fulfilled their ministry—*their* mortal life was soon *ended.* Yet our LORD promises them, saying, "*Lo, I am with you, alway, even unto the end of the world. Amen.*"

How then can this promise be carried on, from generation to generation, even to the end of the world? It is plain that we must understand this promise of our LORD's special Presence with the Eleven, "*even to the end of the world,"* to mean *this*—that our LORD would be present, in a special manner, not merely with those *first Eleven* Ministers of His Grace, but also *with all those who should succeed them* in the ordinary offices of the Christian Ministry, in all ages, even to the end. For it is plain that the Church must have its ministers in *all* ages, as well as at the beginning, and they all require the same special Presence of the LORD to render effectual their ministrations, just as much as the *first* Eleven did. Nothing can ever be *effectually done,* in the ministration of the Word and Sacraments of CHRIST, without His authority and His Presence.

Accordingly we read, in the *Acts* and in the *Epistles* of the holy Apostles, how they ordained others to succeed them in the ordinary offices of the Christian Ministry. They "*ordained Elders,"* it is written, "*in every city."* And S. Paul, we read, ordained *Timothy* to be the first Bishop of Ephesus, and *Titus* to be the first Bishop of Crete; giving them spiritual power and authority to ordain *others* also to *follow them,* warning them to "*lay hands suddenly on no man."*

Thus, before the Apostles left the world, they made a proper provision for the continuation of the Christian Ministry, by continual ordination and succession from themselves even to *the end of the world.* And in this way, brethren, and by this means, the Church has been kept up from that day to this. By this means, Bishops, Priests, and Deacons have been continued in the Church from the time of the Apostles to *our* time.

Nothing has ever been guarded with such great care as this succession from the Apostles has been. So that no one who properly considers the subject can have the slightest shadow of a doubt that the Bishops of the present day have succeeded to their sacred office according to the method appointed by the Apostles; *they* have been ordained by the Bishops before them, and *those* Bishops by the Bishops *before them*, and so on, backwards, till we come to the first Bishops ordained by the Apostles themselves. There is no trace, no hint whatever in the New Testament of *any other* method for making Ministers in the Church of CHRIST than this.

This is the only method, therefore, by which the original commission, given by the LORD Himself, can be handed down from generation to generation, from *that* day to *this;* this is the only way in which the promise of our LORD's special Presence can be claimed, even to the end of the world.

It is true, indeed, that many people in our day, "*having itching ears,*" (as S. Paul well expresses it,) and not "*being able to endure* sound doctrine, heap to themselves teachers," each sect according to its own particular opinions. And many well-meaning people see no harm, no danger, no sin, in all these unhappy divisions. Many think that in Religion *all* have a right to do that which is right in their own eyes. And so all true Christian Unity seems lost from among us; the unity of *Public Worship* is broken all to pieces; the unity of the *Altar of Christ* is entirely overlooked and forgotten; the *unity of the Church of Christ* seems shattered to pieces. We seem to be living in *Babylon*, the city of confusion—not in *Jerusalem*, the City of the Living GOD, the City of Peace and Unity.

I am not presuming, brethren, for a moment to lay the blame of this *here or there;* I am merely stating the fact, and asking you all to lament and deplore it, and to seek and to pray for the restoration of peace and unity again. But this we can never hope for, unless we seek for it *in the ways* that our LORD has appointed and commanded.

Finally, then, brethren, let me beg you to remember, that when I minister to you in sacred things; when I *teach* you in my sacred office; when I *baptize;* when I administer the other Holy Sacrament; I do not do these things *in my own name*—I do them by virtue of the special power given unto me, under the original commandment given by the Divine Head of the Church—*in His Name,* and *for Him.* When the bell rings, and I call you together for Public Worship, I do so "*in the Name of Christ,*" i. e., *with His Authority given unto me.* There is no other Assembly in this village called together "*in the Name of Christ,*" i. e., *by His Authority;* there is no other place but only *the Font* in this Church appointed by Divine authority for this village, at which you can be baptized; there is no other place in this village appointed by Divine authority, but only *the Altar* in this Church, at which you can receive the LORD's Body.

If others pretend to teach you another doctrine; if others pretend to baptize you; if others pretend to give you another Bread—it is all done without any spiritual authority; it is all done *out of unity* with the Church which was established by CHRIST and His Apostles.

For our LORD, we may be very sure, has built His Church, not in division, but in unity. The Divine Head of the Church gave special power and authority, *not* to the disciples at large, but *only to the Eleven and to their successors,* to *teach* and to *baptize* in His Name. And it is our most bounden duty to observe all things whatsoever the LORD hath appointed and commanded.

SERMON XIV.

THE MINISTRY ON EARTH.

EPH. IV. 11, 12.

"AND HE GAVE, SOME APOSTLES, AND SOME PROPHETS, AND SOME EVANGELISTS, AND SOME PASTORS AND TEACHERS; FOR THE PERFECTING OF THE SAINTS, FOR THE WORK OF THE MINISTRY, FOR THE EDIFYING OF THE BODY OF CHRIST."

THESE words of the Apostle evidently set before us, first, the Divine Institution of the Christian Ministry, and then the object of that Institution.

S. Paul had just quoted a verse from the Sixty-eighth Psalm. In the eighteenth verse of that Psalm the prophecy concerning the Ascension of our LORD is this, *"Thou hast ascended on high; Thou hast led captivity captive; Thou hast received gifts for men."*

On the Ascension of the LORD JESUS into the Presence of the FATHER, He received new gifts, and those gifts were *"for men;"* they were for us to share in. The FATHER most highly exalted His SON on His Ascension into His Presence as Man, and He gave unto Him new gifts of power and glory. For instance, *" God gave Him to be the Head over all things, to the Church which is His Body."* As our LORD Himself also declared, just as He was about to ascend, *" All power is given unto Me in heaven and in earth."*

But these new gifts, which the SON of GOD received of the FATHER on His Ascension in our nature into heaven, were *" gifts for men."* They were gifts in which we were to partake, gifts necessary for our salvation; gifts not for the Head of the Body alone to possess, but to be communicated from Him to all His members also. So that we mark that S. Paul in quoting the ancient Prophecy, slightly changes the expression, for he quotes it thus, *" When He ascended up on high, He led captivity captive, and gave gifts unto men,"* because then He began to dispense unto men of those new gifts which He Himself received of the FATHER.

Now therefore let us consider the very first gift which S. Paul mentions, *" And He gave, some Apostles, and some Prophets, and some Evangelists, and some Pastors and Teachers."*

Let us call to mind how this same truth is

declared unto us by the LORD Himself. Being about to ascend to the throne of His glory, He calls together the eleven Disciples, and He speaks to them these words, "*All power is given unto Me in heaven and in earth. Go ye, therefore, and teach all nations, baptizing them in the Name of the Father, and of the Son, and of the Holy Ghost.*"

The very first exercise of our LORD's new power is, we see, thus to commission the eleven, thus to constitute them His Apostles, thus to institute the offices of the Christian Ministry. He Who had loved the Church and given Himself for it, would not ascend into heaven and leave it in this world without supplying it with all needful means for its continual welfare and edification.

For we should certainly mark that *the continuance* of this Divine Institution is essentially implied and absolutely promised in the words of our LORD which follow those just quoted, "*Lo, I am with you, alway, even to the end of the world.*" To the end of the present dispensation of His grace, the ascending LORD promises that His special Presence shall be with the Apostles.

To the end of the world, therefore, we must conclude, there will be persons who succeed the Apostles in the ordinary offices of the Christian

Ministry, with whom the LORD Himself will be specially present, in order to render effectual their ministrations in His Name. And accordingly we read that before they left the world the Apostles made express provision for this continuance of the Christian Ministry. They did not leave the method of continuing it to the will or choice of the people, but they themselves ordained Elders in every city, appointing Deacons also; thus constituting a threefold order, holding the first order themselves. Some were also ordained to succeed themselves in the first order, such as Timothy, the first Bishop of Ephesus, and Titus, the first Bishop of Crete, who had power given them to ordain others also, as the Epistles written to them bear witness. By this method, which was thus begun by the Apostles of CHRIST, the threefold order of the Ministry has been most carefully kept up in the Church from that day to this.

This is the only method recorded in Holy Scripture for the continuance of the Christian Ministry in the world, even to the end. There is no hint of any other method. This is the method by which the Bishops, Priests, and Deacons in the Church have received their spiritual office and authority all along, even to our day.

Thus alone have we received spiritual authority to minister to you, brethren, in the Word and the Sacraments of CHRIST. Our spiritual authority is derived, not in the slightest degree from the Queen or any temporal power, but only from CHRIST Himself, the Divine Head of the Church, by means of this method of continual succession from the Apostles, which the Apostles themselves began, which has been ever since kept up and guarded with the most jealous care in the Church.

Such therefore is the Divine Institution and the Divine authority of the threefold order of the Christian Ministry; and such is the provision made for its continuance in the world, even unto the end of the present dispensation.

The Christian Ministry is a Divine Gift. The first exercise of the new power given to our LORD on His Ascension is to give this gift unto His Church. It is a gift proceeding from those gifts which were then given unto Himself. He being then given to be Head over all things to the Church and our Priest before the FATHER, immediately constitutes the Ministry of His Church on earth, and authorises His Apostles and their successors to the end of the world to speak and to act for Him, to be His Ambassadors, His Priests upon earth, discharging in His Name His Priesthood amongst us here below.

Now let us consider the object for which the Head of the Church has given this Institution to us. It is "*For the perfecting of the Saints, for the work of the Ministry, for the edifying of the Body of Christ.*" For this is certainly needed in every age, and in every nation alike. This is wanted to-day, just as much as it was at the beginning.

It is most true indeed, in spiritual matters, as well as in earthly things, that, "*Neither is he that planteth anything, neither is he that watereth; but God, that giveth the increase.*" Nevertheless we all know, GOD is not wont to give the increase, without the planting and the watering. The excellency of the power is all of GOD. Nevertheless that power is generally exercised by the means and instruments which GOD has been pleased to appoint, even by weak human agents.

The Ministers of CHRIST are labourers employed by GOD, they are His instruments. He is able to render effectual their ministrations. He will most surely make good His own promises; He will bless His own ordinances, and fulfil the purposes for which He appoints them. So that we firmly believe that a faithful use of this gift of CHRIST will issue in the perfecting of the Saints, in the edification of the Body of CHRIST. For this is a channel divinely appointed for our use, through which heavenly grace is ever flowing down from the Head of the Body, for the growth and perfection of all those members of the Body who duly use it.

From these truths then we may make some practical conclusions.

Let me remind you, brethren, that you have as much interest in the Christian Ministry as we have. Rather you have more. We do not speak of this Divine Institution in order to exalt ourselves, but in order to magnify the sacred office which we hold for your sake. It is ordained by CHRIST Himself for your edification, for your perfection. Although we hold an office of spiritual authority, although we are "*set over you in the Lord*," according to the LORD's holy Institution, yet, brethren, we are *your servants*, for CHRIST's sake.

Next, let us consider that if the Divine Head of the Church has been pleased to institute the various Offices of the Christian Ministry, then it certainly follows that every member of the Church is bound to use that Ministry; he is bound to seek for edification and for perfection in the grace of CHRIST, by the use of those Ordinances which CHRIST has appointed for that purpose. No one surely may venture to say that those purposes for which CHRIST has instituted the Christian Ministry shall be accomplished in him as well without the use of those ministrations as with them.

But next, let us ever regard the Office rather than the officer. We are but poor weak earthen vessels in our own selves; but yet an earthen vessel can hold a heavenly treasure, and that treasure, brethren, for you. Look therefore through the weakness of the human instrument, and rest your faith on the Divine Institution, the Divine promise, the Divine presence. Come to Church waiting upon GOD rather than upon man. GOD is able to bless the feeblest instrument for the edification of those who humbly and faithfully wait upon Him in the ways which He has appointed. The unworthiness of the individual Minister does not hinder the grace of CHRIST from those who humbly seek it according to Institutions of CHRIST. In particular, the unworthiness of the individual Minister never hinders the grace of CHRIST in the ministration of those two Holy Sacraments which CHRIST has made necessary for your salvation. Reverence therefore Divine Institutions. Regard the Office rather than the officer. The Christian Ministry is as much of GOD now as the Jewish Ministry was before. The Christian Ministry is as much a Divine gift as the Sacraments are. It is an Institution deriving its origin and authority from the Headship and the Priesthood of our ascended LORD; it is one of the gifts procured for the continual edification of the Church on His Ascension into the Presence of the FATHER.

Lastly, as the work of this Ministry is instituted entirely for your sake, brethren, as our labour in the LORD is entirely for you, one other duty belongs to you respecting it, and that is, that you should maintain your Minister. The precepts of the Gospel are very many and very express on this point. Some of the sentences appointed for use at the Offertory are always sufficient to remind you of this duty. In most parishes, indeed, this duty is sufficiently discharged by the endowment provided. But otherwise, the duty is plainly one of the very first obligation.

SERMON XV.

OUR LORD'S PRIESTHOOD.

HEB. IV. 10.

"WE HAVE A GREAT HIGH PRIEST, THAT IS PASSED INTO THE HEAVENS, JESUS THE SON OF GOD."

CONSIDER the excellency of the Person here spoken of, "*Jesus, the Son of God.*" The title, "*the Son of God,*" denotes His Divine nature. He is of the FATHER, of one substance with the FATHER, not made, nor created, but begotten by an eternal generation. So as that touching His Godhead He could say, "*I and My Father are one.*" In the Unity of one Godhead, therefore, the Person here spoken of is one with the FATHER and the HOLY GHOST, in majesty co-eternal, in glory equal.

But His Name is not only "*the Son of God,*" but also "*Jesus.*" This is the new Name which He now bears for us, taken upon Himself in this lower world, now made a name of power and glory supreme. This Name, literally signifying "*Jah, or Jehovah, a Saviour,*" He received when He was born into this world for our salvation. For He has now taken for ever the Manhood into the Godhead. By the Mystery of the Incarnation He has been made of one substance and nature with us. Here is the grand glory of the human race, that GOD the SON is now for ever "*manifest in the flesh;*" that the Person of whom the Apostle speaks is "*Jesus, the Son of God;*" GOD and Man in one Person.

Next consider the excellency of the Office which He now discharges for us—"*We have a Great High Priest.*" Now the office of a Priest upon earth has been from the beginning ordained of GOD, and it has been ordained, S. Paul writes, "*for the offering of gifts and sacrifices,*" in things pertaining to the service and worship of GOD. But although persons have been taken from among men and called of GOD to the sacred office of Priesthood in the Church on earth, all along, even from the beginning, yet all *they* have served only "*unto the shadow and example of heavenly things.*" A priest in the Church on earth serves only as an example, or pattern, or shadow, or instrument of Him Who alone is a Priest indeed, the one only true

Priest, even our great High Priest, JESUS, the SON of GOD.

The sacred institutions of GOD in His Church on earth are so ordained by Him, as to show forth and represent here below the infinite mysteries and great realities in Heaven above; they are Divinely appointed also to be means and instruments here below connecting us with the very service and worship of Heaven above.

All Priesthood upon earth is thus expressly ordained of GOD for an example or pattern here below of the Priesthood of the SON of GOD Himself in Heaven above. We may humbly believe that in some sense far transcending our knowledge the SON of GOD has been a Priest to the FATHER from all eternity. For the true idea of Priesthood seems involved of necessity in the idea of Sonship.

The present exercise of that eternal Priesthood on our behalf is, so far as we know, only one of its manifold exercises; a new exercise of it, rendered necessary for the salvation of this our fallen world. For in order to our salvation, it was necessary in the order of the Divine Will that the SON of GOD should be made Man; that so He might be fitted to become a Priest for this world. But having thus been made Man, and so being in a condition inferior to the FATHER, the LORD JESUS would not glorify and exalt Himself *by taking upon Himself* this office of a Priest for this world; "*Christ glorified not Himself, to be made an High Priest;*" but He waited until He was outwardly and publicly *called* by the Voice of the FATHER from Heaven at His Baptism, which said, "*Thou art My Son, in Whom I am well pleased.*"

Then, being called by the FATHER, and anointed with the HOLY GHOST to be the CHRIST of GOD, the LORD JESUS began to be our Priest. And then He laid down His Life for us, as both Priest and Victim; giving His Body in sacrifice to the FATHER, in heavenly truth and profound mystery, at the institution of the Holy Eucharist; laying down His Body on the Cross to be crucified and slain; fulfilling all the ancient bloody sacrifices in His own Blood-shedding, making that one only true Sacrifice of Atonement which all they had pointed to and represented from the beginning. And then, forty days after His Resurrection He ascended into Heaven; He went in within the veil, and appeared before the Presence of the FATHER, no longer the SON of GOD only, but Man also, our great High Priest; bringing and carrying in with Him and presenting before the true Mercy-Seat above the Blood of His own Sacrifice, fulfilling the Divinely ordered

Type in heavenly truth and holy mystery; so ever living there, the Priest of this our fallen world, making Intercession for us through His all-atoning Sacrifice.

This brings us to consider, lastly, the excellency of the Place where our great High Priest is now ever ministering for us. He has now "*passed into the Heavens;*" He is now "*made higher than the Heavens;*" He is now "*on the right hand of the throne of the Majesty in the Heavens.*" He is no longer here below, in the weakness of His earthly mortal life. But He is in the true Sanctuary of the highest Heaven, in the power and in the glory of the FATHER, before the true Mercy-Seat of GOD within the vail. He is ever discharging His office on our behalf, as our Priest, at the very Heavenly Altar itself, before the immediate Presence of the Majesty on high.

Such, then, is the excellence of the Person, such the excellence of the Office, and such the excellence of the Place concerning which the text speaks. We now have a Priest ever ministering on our behalf, even before the Presence of the FATHER; and that Priest is One Who is Himself both GOD and Man, having, therefore, as GOD perfect knowledge of the FATHER, and as Man perfect knowledge of us; able, therefore, as GOD to prevail for us with the FATHER, and able also as Man to be touched with a feeling of all our human infirmities, a merciful High Priest, one who is not ashamed to call us His brethren.

Such an Office does the ascended LORD JESUS now discharge continually on our behalf in the highest Heaven. Indeed, all that had been done before, we may say, was in order to this very end. All was done, that the SON of GOD might be fitted and qualified to become our Priest before the FATHER, even a Priest for this fallen world before the throne of the Majesty on high. He, the eternal SON of GOD, was born into this world, He was made partaker of our nature; He received the new Name of JESUS; He made the one all-atoning Sacrifice of Himself for our sins; He rose again from the dead; He ascended and passed into the Heavens: all, in order that He might become fitted and able to be our great High Priest before the very Presence of the FATHER.

Let us then ever praise the Love of GOD towards this fallen world, in thus setting at His own right hand One thus qualified to be our Priest continually before Him. GOD so loved us as to send His SON into the world, to be born into our human family, to be made one with us. GOD so loved us, as to deliver up His SON even unto death, to be made a sacrifice for our sins. GOD so loved us, as to raise up His SON from the dead in our nature, and then to exalt Him in our nature even to His own throne of power and glory. GOD so loved us, as to place His SON, in our nature, at His own right hand, to be our great High Priest, to minister there continually on our behalf. *"Who is he that condemneth? It is Christ that died; yea, rather, that is risen again; Who is even at the right hand of God; Who also maketh intercession for us."*

This is the end and fruit of all that went before, even the present Priesthood of the Ascended LORD JESUS at the right hand of GOD. *"Wherefore He is able to save to the uttermost, seeing He ever liveth to make intercession."*

SERMON XVI.

THE FULFILMENT OF THE ANCIENT TYPE.

HEB. IX. 12.

"BY HIS OWN BLOOD HE ENTERED IN ONCE INTO THE HOLY PLACE."

ALL the ordinances of Divine worship under the Jewish law were so appointed and ordered, through the Divine foreknowledge, that they should be express figures or types of those better things which were promised, which we now possess in the kingdom of the Messiah. So that we observe that when S. Paul would explain to the Hebrews these better things, he explains them by the help of those types or figures of them which were so fore-ordained of GOD through Moses.

The Epistle to the Hebrews contains, chiefly, one great subject, the Priesthood of our LORD. And this subject is explained in this chapter by means of one of the principal types of it which GOD had given in former ages, in the institution of the Jewish Priesthood. In order, therefore, that we may be able to enter into the full meaning of the verse before us, it is quite necessary that we should first of all consider the ancient figure or type to which it refers.

In the Tabernacle which GOD directed Moses to make for the purposes of Divine worship, we must observe that there was, first, the outer court, in which was the altar of burnt sacrifice; then the building itself was divided into two places—the first called the Holy Place, the second, separated by a vail, called the Holy of Holies. In this innermost place there was the Ark of the Covenant, the cover of which was called the Mercy-Seat, which was overshadowed by the Cherubim. Here it was that GOD granted His special Presence, as He said to Moses, *" There will I meet with thee, and I will commune with thee from above the Mercy-Seat."*

Now into the open court, and into the first holy place, all the priests entered continually, accomplishing the services appointed for them. But into the second holy place, the Holy of Holies, which was the more immediate Presence Chamber of GOD, a type or figure of Heaven, no priest might ever enter, except the High

Priest alone, and he only on one day in the year, which was called the Day of Atonement. It is to this entrance of the High Priest into the Holy of Holies once a year that S. Paul especially refers in the chapter before us. He says that it was expressly ordained of GOD to be a figure of the Entrance of our LORD Himself, as our true Priest, into Heaven itself, before the very Presence of the FATHER, on our behalf.

Consider, then, this typical entrance of the Jewish High Priest once a year into the Holy of Holies so expressly ordered by the Divine foreknowledge. It is recorded in Leviticus xvi. He first of all killed the sacrifice at the altar in the outer court. Then he entered in within the vail, before the Mercy-Seat; but "*not without blood,*" on pain of death. He carried in with him the blood of the sacrifice which was slain in the outer court. Then, covering the Mercy-Seat with clouds of incense, he sprinkled the blood of the Sacrifice before the Mercy-Seat and upon the Mercy-Seat seven times. The blood of the sacrifice being thus brought in and offered within the vail, before the special Presence of GOD, according to this Divinely prescribed ritual, the sacrifice itself was completed and accepted, and so atonement was made for the sins of the people for the whole year.

This was the only occasion on which the Blood of the Sacrifice was ever carried in, into the Holy of Holies, and presented before the Mercy-Seat of GOD. This was therefore called the great Day of Atonement, when thus once a year the High Priest alone entered into the Holy of Holies and presented the Blood of the Sacrifice before the special Presence of GOD. This, we may say, completed all the Sacrifices of the whole year. They were all thus presented and accepted in this one. The Blood of this one annual Sacrifice which was thus carried in and offered before the Mercy-Seat, carried in also the Blood of all the Sacrifices of the whole year.

This then is the Type which was expressly ordered by GOD through Moses to be a true Figure upon earth of that Reality itself which is now come in the fulness of time. For the Jewish High Priest in this most solemn action once a year represented Him Who alone is the true Priest. His entrance into the Holy of Holies in the earthly Tabernacle represented the Ascension and entrance of our Great High Priest into the very Presence of the FATHER in Heaven itself. The offering of the Blood of the Sacrifice before and upon the Mercy-Seat was a most striking and expressive figure of the truth and the reality itself which our LORD

The Fulfilment of the Ancient Type. 141

Himself now fulfils before the very Mercy-Seat of GOD in the highest Heaven.

He offered Himself for us "*once for all*," as the Holy Scripture witnesses; but we cannot conceive of things once done in Heaven above otherwise than as essentially continuous without repetition; for repetition of a thing once done belongs only to the accidents of time, not to the conditions of eternity. So then our LORD having been slain in Sacrifice, as the very Lamb of GOD, on the Altar of the Cross, in the outer Court of this lower world, has now ascended and entered in within the vail, appearing in the very Presence of the FATHER as our true Priest, ever ministering for us, fulfilling the Divinely foreordained Type, sprinkling in profound mystery the very Mercy-Seat with the all-atoning Blood of that Sacrifice which He made of Himself in this lower world. For, as the Apostle writes, "*He entered in,*" not with the Blood of those former typical sacrifices, but "*with His own Blood.*" He carried in with Him, in a heavenly mystery, the Blood of His own Sacrifice.

The figure before us teaches us and requires us to distinguish between the Act of *making the Sacrifice* by suffering and by death upon the Cross in this outer world, and the Act of *presenting that Sacrifice* within the vail in the true Holy of Holies above. The Sacrifice is not completed and accepted until it is carried in and presented before the very Mercy-Seat of GOD above.

At the institution of the Holy Eucharist our LORD began the great Act of Sacrifice, for there He began to be our true Melchisedek, offering the Sacrifice of Himself to the FATHER under the earthly elements of Bread and Wine. Then He was slain upon the Cross and suffered death, and shed His most precious all-atoning Blood. There He became the Lamb of GOD slain. And then He ascended and carried in the Blood of the Sacrifice before the true Mercy-Seat of GOD, and offered it upon the Heavenly Altar itself, fulfilling the foreordained Type in heavenly reality.

And here we must also mark the fulfilment of that Type in another particular. Upon the entrance of the Jewish High Priest into the special Presence of GOD, he brought in fire from off the Altar of Burnt Offering, and kindled therewith the clouds of Incense, with which he covered the Mercy-Seat. This was an express Type of those intercessions which our Great High Priest now ever lives to make before the Presence of the FATHER in the true Tabernacle above, on which our final salvation so intimately depends.

The Fulfilment of the Ancient Type. 143

The cloud of Incense kindled with fire from off the Altar of Sacrifice represents those all-prevailing intercessions of our LORD on our behalf, founded upon His own Sacrifice, with which He now ever surrounds the true Mercy-Seat, and by which He procures for us every needful blessing of grace, mercy, and peace.

In the type which was foreordained of GOD, and therefore intended to teach us infallibly the truth on this great matter, we could not say that the slaying of the Sacrifice in the outer court was sufficient, without its presentation within the vail, and without the cloud of Incense covering the Mercy-Seat. Even so in the Antitype, the great reality itself; we dare not venture to say that the slaying of the Sacrifice on the Cross in this world is sufficient, without its presentation in Heaven itself by our Great High Priest, and without His continual intercessions founded thereupon before the Presence of the FATHER.

The Death on the Cross was the slaying of the Sacrifice; now our LORD has "*entered in, not with the blood of bulls and of goats, but with His own Blood,*" by means of which He now intercedes for us, ever ministering for us in His Priestly Office.

The work which CHRIST began for us upon earth in humiliation and in weakness, and which He finished here below, being slain in Blood and Death, He now ever lives to carry on for us in infinite power and glory above, our True Priest, ever ministering for us in the Presence of the FATHER, appearing under the form of a Lamb, which had been the sacrificial animal all along; presenting Himself as "*the Lamb slain,*" bearing in His Body before the FATHER the very marks of His crucifixion; pleading for us His all-atoning Death, ever presenting, in heavenly reality, that one eternal Sacrifice which He once made of Himself in this outer world, and so interceding for us.

The Sacrifice was slain in this world, and it is now carried in by the Great High Priest of the Church, and so completed and accepted, being offered within the vail, at the heavenly Altar, before the true Mercy-Seat of GOD. Hence it is that we read such words as these, "*Who is he that condemneth? It is Christ that died; yea, rather, that is risen again, Who is even at the right hand of God, Who also maketh intercession for us.*" And "*Wherefore He is able to save to the uttermost all that come unto God by Him, seeing He ever liveth to make intercession for them.*" And also, "*If, when we were enemies, we were reconciled unto God by His Death, much more,*

The Fulfilment of the Ancient Type. 145

being reconciled, we shall be saved by His Life."

One more truth, closely connected with this subject, let us briefly call to mind.

That which our Great High Priest is ever doing for us Himself in heaven above, He has commanded us also to be ever doing here upon earth; not according to our own inventions, but in heavenly mysteries, according to His express Institution. For He has Himself furnished His Church on earth with the proper and special means of doing this, by instituting for us the peculiar and proper means of uniting our worship below with His own ministrations above. He has made the Holy Eucharist to be the one distinctive act of worship for the whole Church on earth till He come again. In this, we do upon earth, by His command and through His Priesthood, the very same thing, in meaning and in intention, which He is doing in Heaven; we present in holy mysteries the LORD's atoning Death, we plead the LORD's one eternal Sacrifice.

Rather, our Great High Priest Himself is present, and beneath all the outward elements, and under all the human instruments, He Himself is the ministering Priest, and by this His own Divine Service He lifts up all into heaven itself, and presents our worship at the heavenly

Altar, and procures for us the blessings of His saving grace.

If we may speak in human words apart from the accidents of time, we may express this innermost heavenly reality under the conceptions designedly suggested by the divinely given type of former ages, and say, that at this the LORD's own most special Service, we call into special exercise His Priestly ministrations; and whilst we are praying in the outer courts of His Church, He Himself is offering the Blood of His Sacrifice within the vail, on the heavenly Altar above, and prevailing, on our behalf, with His all-acceptable intercessions, founded on that all-atoning Sacrifice.

For then, if at any moment, the Type must be fulfilled; then the Blood is sprinkled on the Mercy-Seat; then the cloud of incense covers the Altar within the vail.

For when we "*do this*" upon earth by our LORD's own express command, and in the very way He has appointed for us, He Himself makes effective His own ordinances. If He "*ever lives*" to discharge His Priestly Office on our behalf, surely He does so on this occasion in some special manner.

Thus we learn that this is our chief Service upon earth. In this Service heaven and earth are united in one. This Service is the same, in its most essential nature, as that which our Great High Priest Himself ever discharges above.

Here therefore we should ever count it our most blessed privilege to join our worship with that above, through the Priestly Office of our LORD before the Presence of the FATHER.

SERMON XVII.

THE PRIESTLY MINISTRATIONS.

HEBREWS VIII. 1, 2.

"WE HAVE SUCH A HIGH PRIEST, WHO IS SET ON THE RIGHT HAND OF THE THRONE OF THE MAJESTY IN THE HEAVENS, A MINISTER OF THE SANCTUARY AND OF THE TRUE TABERNACLE."

THESE words set before us one of the very chief Articles of the Christian Revelation, the present Priesthood of our ascended SAVIOUR.

We are perhaps accustomed to think too exclusively of our LORD's life in this world eighteen hundred years ago. We do not sufficiently consider our LORD's present life in heaven. We remember that our LORD died for us, but we do not sufficiently remember that He is now ever living for us. We remember His former life of humiliation and weakness and suffering here below, but we too much forget

His present life of glory and of power in heaven above.

If our LORD had never ascended into heaven as Man, if He were not now our ever-living Priest before the Mercy-Seat of GOD, it would make but little difference in the faith of many. We believe in the LORD JESUS as our Redeemer, but we do not sufficiently believe in Him as our Priest, now continually exercising His office of a Priest for us in the true Sanctuary above, our everliving Intercessor. We do not sufficiently consider that all that our SAVIOUR did for us here below is now rendered effectual, and applied to us, by His present life in heaven, through the continual discharge of His Priestly office. Indeed, all that our LORD did and suffered here below was in preparation for His Priestly office above.

He laid down His Body on the Altar of the Cross, in the outer court of this world, to suffer death once for all in pain and blood, in order that He might have an infinitely precious and all-atoning Sacrifice, to present and plead continually within the vail before the true Mercy-Seat of GOD, where He now abideth a Priest continually. This present Priesthood of our LORD at the right hand of the Throne of the Majesty in the Heavens is the end, this is the very fruit of all that is gone before. It is very certain therefore that we should frequently consider and firmly believe this most fundamental and vital truth of the Christian religion.

Our LORD is now given to us as *our Priest*. "*We have such a High Priest;*" He is *ours*, in this Office; it is for us and for our salvation that He holds and continually exercises the office of a Priest before the FATHER. For through the discharge of this office it is that He is now able to save to the uttermost all that come unto GOD by Him.

"*He now ever liveth to make intercession for us.*" He is now therefore ever taking away the sins of the world. If any man sin, He is the propitiation for our sin. In every hour of need He is ready to send us help from above. He is ever ready to minister for each one of us, through His all-prevailing intercession.

All the mercies, blessings, graces, and gifts which we have or pray for, which are necessary for our present and eternal salvation, *all* come to us through the continual ministrations of our Great High Priest at the right hand of the FATHER.

All our worship here below, all our prayers and praises, all our offerings and services, *all* are offered to the FATHER, *all* are accepted by Him, only as they are presented by the hands of our Great High Priest, cleansed by His Sacrifice, made acceptable by His merits and intercessions.

"*We have such a High Priest;*" we all have such a Priest; His Priesthood is for us *all* to benefit by; He belongs to us *all* in this office: He now ever lives to discharge His Priestly office for *all* of us, yea, even for every one of us, even for the lowest and weakest member. Not *one* is overlooked by Him. As He once *died* for all, so now He ever *lives* for all. His present life in glory is devoted to our service.

We read in the Gospels, that once when the LORD JESUS was walking along the road on His last journey to Jerusalem to suffer death on the Cross, a certain poor blind man sitting by the wayside begging, cried unto Him in faith and patience, and the LORD JESUS "*stood still*" at the voice of his prayer, and granted him all his petition. And is the same LORD less full of pity now? Is He less ready to hear a sinner's cry now? Is He moved with compassion for our bodily afflictions, and not much more for our spiritual? Surely our Great High Priest did those things amongst us here upon earth on purpose to teach us His goodness toward us, and His perfect readiness to listen to any sinner's cry. Such as the LORD

Jesus was then to that poor blind man, such is He now also to all who call upon Him in faith and patience.

And now He is never wearied any more with the concourse of people seeking His help, never tired any more with the multitude of sick folk who call upon Him. As He stood still to listen to the cry of that poor blind man, although on His way to be crucified, so does the same Lord Jesus still attend to the wants of all who seek His grace, in His perfect Divine charity.

If therefore any of us, even the humblest and the weakest, in any time of need, earnestly cry unto Him from the depth of our affliction, believing in Him, putting all our trust and confidence in His ever-living intercession before the Father, He is ready to minister for us as our compassionate High Priest; He is ready and able to attend to the wants of each one in His Divine charity, just as perfectly as if that one were the only one who required His attention.

If any of us, even the least and weakest believer, bring any worship, any act of faith or of love, any service, any offering unto God, then does our Great High Priest above execute His Priestly office, and presents that service or worship, or offering, before the Mercy-Seat of God, making it acceptable through the sweet perfume of the incense of His own Intercessions, through the virtue of His own Sacrifice.

If ever a poor widow, in faith and love towards her SAVIOUR and her GOD, casts into the LORD's treasury a grateful offering, even only of two mites, even of all her living, then does the Great High Priest above execute His priestly office, and lifts the acceptable offering into the Presence of the FATHER, and changes the two mites below into a mountain of gold, making them rich, and costly, and precious in His sight, through the virtue of His own Sacrifice and Intercession.

If only two or three are gathered together in His Name to offer worship and service, then, according to His own special promise, our Great High Priest discharges His priestly office, and presents the service before the Majesty on High.

If a trembling repenting sinner truly turns unto GOD, and mourns with godly sorrow for his sins, and yields himself a living sacrifice unto GOD, as one alive from the dead, then does our gracious and compassionate High Priest execute His office above, and offers the sacrifice of that broken and contrite heart, the tears of that godly sorrow, before the throne of Mercy in the highest heavens, and procures for that penitent sinner pardon and peace, through the virtue of His own all-atoning Sacrifice.

Above all, when according to His own command, we meet together in Church to show the LORD's Death, to present the one only Sacrifice, in sacred memorial, before the eyes of the FATHER, (which is the very soul and centre of all our Christian worship,) then, most especially, is He Himself present, our true Priest, and by the ministry of His appointed Priest on earth He makes good His own Divine words, He renders effectual His own Divine Institution, He lifts up the Memorial to the heavenly Altar, He presents the one all-atoning Sacrifice before the FATHER. In the language of the ancient Type, foreordained by Himself, He sprinkles the Blood of the Sacrifice on the Mercy-Seat of GOD; and so He procures for all faithful worshippers, a participation in that Sacrifice, unto the glories of an unspeakable exaltation. Because in every celebration of that Holy Eucharist, *we* do here below, by our LORD's own command, and in the very way which He Himself appointed, the very thing which He Himself our Great High Priest, is doing in the sanctuary of the highest heaven; we show forth the Sacrifice of the LORD's Death, we lift the eternal and infinite Sacrifice, in union with the heavenly reality above, before the eyes of the

FATHER; believing in, trusting in, pleading by, praying by, our LORD's Priesthood in the Presence of the FATHER.

In all these ways it is permitted us to call into exercise the office of our Great High Priest above. Ever ready, ever willing is the LORD JESUS to minister for us as our Priest before the FATHER.

Here is a gift, a blessing, and an advantage more precious than we can ever rightly value. He is now ever living for us our Priest before the FATHER; ever ready, ever willing, in infinite power and in Divine Charity, to execute His Priestly Office, and to lift up the voice of His all-prevailing intercessions before the true Mercy-Seat above, even for the humblest, the poorest, the weakest, and the most unworthy.

Let us therefore avail ourselves of this season of grace and mercy, now that we have such a High Priest, one with the FATHER, and one with us, ever ministering in our behalf in the true Sanctuary above before the Presence of the FATHER. Let us ever exercise a firm and lively faith in this great Article of the Christian Revelation. Let it be in our mind every time we pray.

SERMON XVIII.

THE CONTINUAL MINISTRATIONS.

HEB. VII. 25.

"HE EVER LIVETH TO MAKE INTERCESSION."

THERE is no greater doctrine in the Christian religion than this. The same LORD JESUS, who once lived, and died, and rose again, in this world, now "*ever liveth,*" even before the Presence of the Eternal FATHER, "*our great High Priest,*" continually "*to make Intercession*" for us.

The *only word* which we will now consider is this word "*ever,*" thus used by S. Paul, "He *ever* liveth to make Intercession." When our LORD was upon the earth in the days of His humiliation, He was subject to human infirmities. On one occasion, S. Mark writes, the multitude that came together was so great, that "*they had no leisure so much as to eat;*" so that our LORD said to His disciples, "*Come ye yourselves apart into a desert place, and rest a while.*" Doubtless the LORD Himself would be *wearied* in attending to so many applicants, not being willing to send even *one* of them empty away. On another occasion, S. John relates, our LORD, "*being wearied with His journey,*" sat on the well at Sychar.

In the days of His flesh here upon earth our LORD was thus *subject to human infirmity*, even as we are. But *now* all weakness is gone; *now* the days of His humiliation are all past. Now "*all power is given unto Him.*" Now "*He ever liveth*" in power and in glory, to minister on our behalf, *our great High Priest*, before the Presence of the FATHER. Now He is no more wearied with the great number of those who call upon Him for help. He never tires, never stops, never is unwilling, never is unable; but "*He ever liveth,*" our *merciful* and our *faithful* Priest, in the very Presence of the FATHER, "*to make Intercession*" for us.

When our LORD was upon earth, as Man, He most willingly and graciously attended to *all* that sought His help; but then He did so for *one only at a time.* He healed them, every one, as first *one* and then *another*, was brought into His Presence and laid down at His feet.

But *now* the LORD is able to be present everywhere throughout His Church at the same time; *now* He is able to attend *to all* equally and perfectly at the same time.

Our great High Priest is ready to minister, in His Office before the Presence of GOD, on behalf of *any one* of us, at *any time, whenever* we draw near to the Throne of Grace, in any and every hour of need. Now "*He abideth a Priest continually.*" *Now* He is *ever* able, *ever* willing, *ever* ready, *ever* waiting, to attend to the wants of *each one* of His disciples, just as easily, just as perfectly, as if *that one* were the *only one* who required His attention. *Ever* is He ready to discharge His Priestly office *for us all*, even for His poorest and weakest disciple, in perfect compassion, in Divinest charity, in infinite power, before the FATHER; *ever* is He ready to fulfil His Office *as our Priest;* *ever* ready to lift the one eternal Sacrifice before the eyes of GOD the FATHER, and through the infinitely precious Blood of that Sacrifice, to make all-prevailing Intercession for us; that we may receive, each one of us, grace, mercy, and peace, according to all our sad necessities.

Call to mind for a moment, brethren, one little incident which occurred one day when our LORD was walking along the road on His last journey to Jerusalem to sacrifice Himself there for our sins. He heard the *voice of a poor blind man*, who was sitting alone by the wayside begging. I need not now relate to you the whole story; but at the cry of this poor blind man, at the voice of his patient earnest prayer, the LORD JESUS "*stood still.*" He could not go by until He had attended to that poor helpless blind man, and relieved him of his sad distress, and filled his heart with light and gladness.

This, Brethren, is a little picture here down upon earth, of what the *same Lord Jesus*, in His perfect charity, is still *ever* doing, in His Priestly Office, in the very Presence of the FATHER. He is *ever* listening to our prayers, never turning a deaf ear even to *one* cry; *ever* ready to minister for us, and unto us; to send us help from above. *Whenever* you draw near unto GOD then, brethren, in any time of need, be sure that you bear in mind *this present truth*. Draw near with a firm and lively faith in the *present Office* of our LORD as OUR PRIEST BEFORE THE FATHER. *Ever pray in His Name,* ever draw near unto GOD, "*by Him,*" *i. e.*, with your faith resting upon His *Mediation,* His *Priesthood;* that all your prayers may be accepted THROUGH HIS INTERCESSION.

But now, brethren, if our LORD is thus *ever*

living, as our *Priest,* before the true Mercy-Seat of GOD above; if He is *ever* ready to discharge His Priestly Office on our behalf before the very Presence of the FATHER; we must certainly believe that He is most especially ready to intercede for us when we assemble and meet together for *that very special Service and worship which is the only one instituted and commanded by Himself,* to " *show the Lord's death*" before the FATHER, according to the way enjoined upon us by the LORD Himself; to plead the Sacrifice of His SON before the FATHER *in a way* in which we can at no other time and by no other means. For it is in this holy service we must ever remember that our great High Priest exercises His Priestly Office for us, as our Priest *according to the Order of Melchisedek,* bringing forth to us *Bread* and *Wine,* by means of which earthly elements He conveys to us in this Holy Sacrament *That* which is Meat indeed, and *That* which is Drink indeed.

In this Holy and only Divine service, brethren, we call into exercise, in the most special manner possible, the Priesthood of our LORD. Whilst *we* below, according to His own Institution, are showing forth His Death, and *doing this* for a memorial of His Sacrifice before the FATHER, behold, *He Himself,* within the vail,

M

shows forth the same Sacrifice above, and covers the Mercy-Seat with the cloud of the incense of His Intercessions, procuring for all true worshippers mercy and grace unto eternal life.

Let us, then, now proceed with this Divine service, this holy *Memorial* of the LORD's atoning Sacrifice, this *Holy Communion* of His life-giving *Body and Blood,* putting *all our trust and confidence* in the continual ministrations of our great High Priest before the very Presence of the FATHER.

SERMON XIX.

THE ORDER OF MELCHISEDEK.

PSALM CX. 4.

"THE LORD SWARE AND WILL NOT REPENT; THOU ART A PRIEST FOR EVER, AFTER THE ORDER OF MELCHISEDEK."

THIS Psalm is remarkable, as containing some of the chief Prophecies concerning our SAVIOUR. It is quoted as such in the writings of the New Testament. The first verse of this Psalm contains that very singular and clear Prophecy of the exaltation of the LORD, the Messiah, to the Throne of the FATHER, which is referred to by S. Paul, by S. Peter, and by our SAVIOUR Himself. "*The Lord said unto my Lord, Sit Thou on My right hand, until I make Thine enemies Thy footstool.*"

In the fourth verse, the Prophecy relates to the Priesthood of the Messiah; "*Thou art a*

Priest for ever." The LORD, the Messiah, is thus therefore constituted both King and Priest. On His Ascension into the Presence of the FATHER, He was given to be the Head over all things to the Church, the King of Glory, having all Power committed to Him both in Heaven and on earth; and at the same time also He began to be our Priest in the Presence of the FATHER.

Let us now mark more particularly this most ancient and remarkable Prophecy concerning the present Priesthood of our LORD.

Here is an absolute Divine decree, ordained by GOD the FATHER, according to the good pleasure of His Will; "*The Lord sware, and will not repent.*" The LORD JEHOVAH, that is GOD the FATHER, thus declares to us His own absolute Will. He reveals to the world this His immutable decree, in the most solemn manner possible; for He confirms it by an Oath. It is as if He had said, "*As I live.*" As S. Paul writes, "*Because He could swear by no greater, He sware by Himself.*" This Revelation is doubtless made in this manner, *under the form of an Oath*, for the strong assurance of our faith; because it is indeed a matter on which rests our very Salvation. GOD, therefore, condescends to assure us of it in the most solemn manner that He could.

What then is the purport of this absolute decree of the Will of the FATHER, thus so solemnly revealed to us? It is this; "*Thou art a Priest for ever after the Order of Melchisedek.*" The Person here addressed is the Person of the Messiah, whose Exaltation to the Throne of the FATHER is foretold in the beginning of the Psalm. Here He is constituted, "*a Priest for ever,*" by the immutable decree of the FATHER.

Of the fulfilment of this Prophecy S. Paul writes; "*Now of the things which we have spoken, this is the sum. We have such an High Priest, Who is set on the right hand of the Throne of the Majesty in the Heavens ; a Minister of the Sanctuary and of the true Tabernacle.*" There He now abideth *a Priest continually;* ever living to minister on our behalf as our Priest before the FATHER. There He ever liveth, our Great High Priest, to make intercession for us, our Mediator and Advocate with the FATHER.

There is nothing in this Divine Revelation, we may observe by the way, which hinders us from believing that GOD the SON exercised an Office, which we may call the Office of a Priest, and which was the very foundation of this His present Priesthood on our behalf, even from all eternity. For it seems that the Sonship involves the Priesthood. The constitution of a Priesthood among men, by Divine appointment, seems only a shadow upon earth of some Original Eternal reality. So that the present exercise of Priesthood by the ascended Incarnate LORD may be, very probably, only some modification of His Eternal Priesthood, only some new exercise of that Priesthood, which is suitable and necessary for the restoration of this our fallen world.

But however this be, the Revelation is most expressly and distinctly given to us, that now, on His Ascension in our nature into the Presence of the FATHER, our LORD began to fulfil the ancient types of His Priesthood, and especially, this most remarkable Prophecy of that Priesthood now under consideration. He then began to be, in a way in which He had never been before, a Priest before the FATHER for this fallen world. For then, no longer as GOD only, but as Man also, He is constituted "*a Priest for ever.*"

But there is another Divinely revealed truth, in the passage before us. It is this; that our LORD's Priesthood is now a Priesthood "*after the Order of Melchisedek.*" The absolute will and eternal decree of the FATHER, is, that the LORD CHRIST should be a Priest before Him for ever, and that that Priesthood should be a

Priesthood, not according to the Order of Aaron, but rather according to the Order of Melchisedek. This truth S. Paul particularly dwells upon, in the seventh chapter of his Epistle to the Hebrews.

In order, then, that we may rightly understand what is here intended, concerning the nature of our LORD's present Priesthood, it is of course necessary that we should carefully consider all that Holy Scripture tells us concerning Melchisedek, who was Priest of the Most High GOD, as well as a King.

It will be sufficient for our present consideration, if we dwell on one distinguishing difference between the Priesthood after the Order of Aaron and the Priesthood after the Order of Melchisedek. Aaron's Priesthood was of course one type and representation upon earth of our LORD's essential Priesthood, and as such it was perfectly fulfilled by our LORD Who was and is our true Aaron, now gone in within the veil, our Great High Priest, "*with His own Blood,*" to sprinkle therewith, in profound reality, the very Heavenly Altar itself, according to the ancient type. But in another respect, our LORD's present Priesthood is rather according to the Order of Melchisedek.

To understand one most essential characteristic of this Priesthood, therefore, we must mark that it is related concerning Melchisedek, that in the one only Priestly action that is recorded of him, (and purposely only *one* such Priestly action is recorded of him,) *he brought forth Bread and Wine*. Now whenever Aaron came forth in *his* Priestly Office to minister before GOD, he brought forth some appointed animal, by means of which he offered his Sacrifice. This was the chief distinctive Sacrifice after the Order of Aaron. By means of some slain animal, he showed forth the one Great Sacrifice which was coming. By means of some animal consumed by fire on the altar of burnt-offering, Aaron's Priesthood sent up a holy Memorial of the Sacrifice of the Lamb of GOD unto the FATHER, and so obtained blessing for the people of GOD.

But Melchisedek, the Royal Priest, blesses the Father of the faithful, *bringing forth Bread and Wine* as the earthly elements of his Sacrifice; he offered no bloody sacrifice; he brought forth only the fruits of the earth, and those fruits, types and representatives of all the rest. Here, therefore, is one essential point, typical and prophetical of the Order of our LORD's Priesthood.

When, then, let us now consider, did the LORD CHRIST Himself introduce this New Order of the Priesthood? When did He begin to execute His own Priesthood, after this Order of Melchisedek? Very plainly on the very day on which He was Himself slain in Sacrifice for the sins of the world. On the evening of that day, after He had celebrated for the last time the ancient Jewish Passover, He put an end to the Priesthood after the Order of Aaron, and began the Priesthood after the Order of Melchisedek. For then the LORD Himself appears in His Priestly Office, as our true Melchisedek, for the first time, bringing forth to us Bread and Wine; using these Fruits of the earth alone, in the most peculiar and remarkable way; sanctifying them to heavenly ends; using them as the earthly materials, by means of which He presents the Sacrifice of Himself to the FATHER; by means of which also He makes us to be partakers of that Sacrifice.

And whatever this Holy Institution was at its first Celebration, such it remains in all generations of the Church; whatever it was then to the first disciples, such it is now to us.

In this Divine Institution then our Great High Priest now continually discharges His office according to the New Order of Melchisedek, bringing forth to us Bread and Wine, making these fruits of the earth to be the distinctive materials for the one distinctive Rite of the New Dispensation. For we must ever bear in mind that our LORD Himself is now present throughout His whole Church. He is not *so* present at the right hand of the FATHER in Heaven itself, as to be absent from His Church on earth. He is ever discharging His Priestly Office in Heaven above, in His own Person, and He is also ever discharging that Office in the Church on earth, in the person of His ministers, to whom He has given the special promise, "*Lo, I am with you always, to the end of the world.*" For our LORD, as a Priest after the Order of Melchisedek, we must remember, discharges His Office here upon earth; for in Heaven itself, it is plain, He does not bring forth Bread and Wine.

Three practical conclusions let us make from this doctrine, thus Divinely revealed to us, concerning our LORD's present Priesthood.

One is this. If we refuse or neglect the very Service instituted for our continual use by our LORD Himself, as indeed the one most distinctive Service of the present Dispensation, in which He Himself, for us and with us, discharges His Priesthood according to the Order of Melchisedek, what do we do but refuse or neglect our LORD's very Priesthood itself in one of its most peculiar and distinctive exercises? And this surely must be very dangerous for us. For what can be the value of our faith or our trust in the Mediation and Priesthood of our LORD, whilst we are wilfully and carelessly neglecting this His own positive Institution, which is the very means and the only means which is positively appointed and ordained by Himself, by which He Himself exercises His Priesthood amongst us here below, according to the Order of Melchisedek?

Another conclusion is this. Whenever we join in the Celebration of this Holy Mystery it is on the invisible Priest that we should earnestly fix our faith,—not on the human minister, who is only the visible hand, the earthly instrument, of the true and only Priest. For in His Own most holy Service the LORD CHRIST is ever Himself specially present in the person of His ministering servants, discharging in it by their means His own Priesthood, bringing forth to us Bread and Wine, blessing and sanctifying these earthly Fruits to holy, spiritual, and heavenly uses. In this holy Mystery it is, that, in the most special way, our worship on earth is joined with the worship above, through the ministrations of our Great High Priest, Who is both there and here present. In this Service it is, more than in any other, that we call into action our LORD's Priesthood according to the Order of Melchisedek. On Him, therefore, whenever we join in its celebration, our whole faith should be firmly and earnestly fixed.

And the third conclusion is this. How unspeakable is our privilege and our blessing that we should thus have a Service appointed for us, not by man's device, but by the LORD Himself, in which we know and are sure that the LORD Himself is specially present, and in which He Himself specially discharges for us His own Priestly Office as a Priest after the Order of Melchisedek, in which Service indeed all who take part are in some true and real sense Priests unto GOD,—all offering unto the FATHER, in union with the Priesthood of CHRIST, the one all-atoning Sacrifice which taketh away the sins of the world.

Here then let us ever esteem it our first duty and our highest privilege to draw near unto GOD by Him Whom He hath constituted our Priest for ever, in the very way which He has appointed for us.

SERMON XX.

OUR PRESENT STATE.

Eph. ii. 6.

"AND HATH RAISED US UP TOGETHER, AND MADE US SIT TOGETHER, IN HEAVENLY PLACES, IN CHRIST JESUS."

The first thing that we should mark in these words is that the Apostle uses the past tense. He does not say that God will raise us up and will make us sit together with Christ, in the world to come, but he writes that God hath raised us up together with Christ, and that He hath made us sit together with Him in heavenly places.

Although our resurrection and our ascension into Glory are certainly future events, yet the Apostle here speaks of them as already in some sense accomplished. They are parts of that great salvation which God has prepared for us, which are yet to come; but nevertheless we are here said to be in some sense already made partakers of them.

Let us then endeavour to understand the true meaning of this statement. For this purpose we must consider that at the Advent of the SON of GOD in the flesh a New Order of things began, a New Kingdom of GOD was established. Of this the holy Baptist gave very clear warning, when he preached, saying, "*Repent, for the Kingdom of Heaven is at hand.*" He called the people to repentance, in order that they might be prepared to enter into that New Kingdom of Heaven which the promised Messiah was just about to set up.

For how could it be that the Eternal SON of GOD should Himself take our human nature and yet all things remain as they were? How could it be, that the Second Person in the Eternal Godhead should be made the New Man, and man not be thereby unspeakably elevated? How could the LORD from Heaven dwell among us here below, and Heaven itself not be brought down to us? How could the Incarnate Word ascend up into Heaven, and be seated on the Throne of the FATHER in our nature, and the world below be left as He found it?

Accordingly, the fruit of all that had gone before, we may say, consisted in the coming down of the HOLY GHOST to begin a New Dispensation of Grace upon earth, to begin that very Kingdom of Heaven upon earth of which the Baptist had spoken as close at hand in his day,—in one word, to open the Kingdom of Heaven upon earth to all believers. So that all things have now been changed to us through the Incarnation, the Sacrifice, the Resurrection, and the Ascension of the SON of GOD in our nature. Now there is in the world a New Kingdom of Heaven, reaching down to us from the Throne of our ascended and glorified LORD.

Into this New Kingdom of GOD were the three thousand converts admitted on the Day of Pentecost; and into the same Kingdom of Heaven have all been admitted ever since who have been baptized; for "*by one Spirit are we all baptized into one Body.*" For the holy Sacrament of Baptism remains the same from age to age; it is the same for every individual; and in it, by a New Birth of Water and the HOLY GHOST, we all enter into the Kingdom of GOD, being made members of the Second Adam, the LORD Incarnate, our New Divine Head.

It is to this, our present gift of GOD's grace, that the Apostle refers in the text, saying, that GOD hath already raised us up together with

CHRIST, and that He hath already made us sit together with Him in heavenly places. By Baptism (as S. Paul writes to the Romans and to the Colossians) we have been buried together with CHRIST, in which Holy Sacrament also we have been raised up together with Him. For, in other words, by the peculiar and special grace belonging to that Sacrament of CHRIST we have been made therein members of CHRIST—members of a risen, an ascended, a glorified Head; we have been united to One Who is already risen and ascended into glory; we have been already made partakers, in some most real and true sense, of the Resurrection and of the Ascension of our Divine Head; we have been incorporated into a new Mystical Body, of which the Head is exalted to the Throne of Glory; we have been entered into the New Kingdom of GOD Incarnate, a kingdom which reaches down from His Throne of Glory and is amongst us here below—a kingdom in this world though not of this world.

But all this, although a present, most true, and real exaltation, is not perceived by sight or sense, but only by faith. The Kingdom of GOD is not yet come with observation of this world; its presence amongst us is as yet known only by faith in the word of CHRIST. But, by faith in that word, we know that we have now come, as S. Paul writes to the Hebrews, unto the true Mount Sion, and unto the City of the Living God, the Heavenly Jerusalem, and to an innumerable company of angels, to the general Assembly and Church of the first-born which are written in Heaven, and to God the Judge of all, and to the spirits of just men made perfect, and to JESUS the Mediator of the New Covenant.

This is the New Kingdom of God into which we have now come—the New Gift of the Ascension of God Incarnate and of the coming down of the HOLY GHOST. Now, through faith, we understand that we are living in the Kingdom of Heaven upon earth. Thus, then, CHRIST our LORD has provided His disciples with *a Heavenly Home for their souls,* even in the midst of all the changes and trials of this world.

This world is no home for our souls. Whatever comforts or gifts it may have to give us, yet they are only for a moment, they are only conveniences and refreshments for our journey through the world; they cannot support and comfort our souls; they will be all quickly stripped away from us. And in how many things the world is an *enemy* to our souls, blinding us with its vanities, stealing our hearts away from GOD, deadening our souls by its deceitful lusts, it is not needful now to consider.

We need something better, something stronger, something nearer to us, than the world. We need something to connect us with the eternal Heaven, with GOD our Maker and our SAVIOUR. And this our LORD has provided for us by leaving amongst us *His Kingdom*, by constituting upon earth *His Church*, which is "*built upon the foundation of the Apostles and Prophets, Jesus Christ Himself being the chief corner-stone.*" The Church of CHRIST is His Mystical Body, which He so loved, and for which He gave Himself; *the One only Brotherhood*, which we are all expressly commanded to *love*. This is the Sign, and Token, and Pledge, and Institution of the Presence of CHRIST amongst us; this is that Divine Communion in which have lived all the Saints of CHRIST; this is the Home of our souls, even in the midst of this present world.

Blessed are they who through faith perceive that the Church of CHRIST is in the world,— that the Kingdom of Heaven is amongst us,— and who dwell in it, as the only home of their souls. As it is written,—"*Blessed are they that dwell in Thy House; they will be always praising Thee.*" Such will be able to say, "*Our conversation is in Heaven;*" they will feel themselves to be citizens of an invisible but eternal kingdom—the kingdom of Christ—which now reaches down from His Throne of glory, and is come even to us, and is amongst us, although without observation of sight and sense, yet prized and loved through faith in the words of Christ.

Let us learn, then, to realize, by faith, the presence of the New Kingdom of God. Let us believe the words of Holy Scripture concerning our present exaltation into the Kingdom of Heaven. For God "*hath raised us up together with Christ, and made us sit together with Him in heavenly places.*" Let us take our thoughts and affections off from this present fleeting world, which is perishing, which cannot bless us, cannot support us, and fix them on the everlasting kingdom of Christ, into which we have already been lifted up together with *Him* Who is our New Divine all-glorious Head. Let us prize the blessings of this kingdom above everything else. Let us seek for a more believing perception of them. Let us pray for the increase of grace, that we may walk worthy of our position in the Church of the Living God, lest, at last, the Judge of all men should cast us out of His Kingdom as evil. Let us bear in mind the voice of warning given by the Church at Ascensiontide,—"*The end of all things is at hand;*" nothing more is to be revealed; nothing more is to be done for us; the full dispensation of grace is with us; now nothing remains, but "*the end of all things.*"

Let us therefore be *earnestly preparing for that day of Glory*, when the sons of GOD, who are now hidden from the knowledge of the world, shall be openly manifested; when the Kingdom of CHRIST shall be revealed in all its Divine Power and Glory; when there will be no more any *trying of our faith;* but we shall see the Incarnate SON of GOD *as He is;* and the open vision of His glory will change *us* also into His Divine Image; and "*so shall we ever be with the Lord.*"

In one word, let the conclusion of the whole matter be this,—"*Since ye are risen with Christ, seek those things which are above, where Christ sitteth on the right hand of God. Set your affection on things above, not on things on the earth. For ye are dead, and your life is hid with Christ in God. When Christ, Who is our Life, shall appear, then shall ye also appear with Him in Glory.*"

SERMON XXI.

THE PROMISE OF OUR ASCENDED LORD.

Rev. iii. 21.

"To him that overcometh will I grant to sit with Me in My throne; even as I also overcame, and am set down with My Father in His throne."

At this season of the Christian Year the Church directs our thoughts to the most glorious and triumphant Ascension of our LORD into the Heaven of heavens. Of all the great events which we celebrate in the whole course of the Christian year relating to GOD our SAVIOUR, *this* is the most full of glory, this is the fruit and the crown of them all, when we celebrate the Ascension of GOD the SON made Man into the glory of the highest Heaven.

Great indeed was "*the Mystery of Godliness,*" when GOD the Eternal SON was manifest in the flesh at His holy *Nativity*, born in a stable, laid in the manger, in great humility indeed.

Great was the mystery of godliness when the LORD from Heaven was seen of the Angels here below living in an estate of great poverty, made even lower than themselves, exposed in this world to weakness, temptation, contempt and affliction.

Great was the mystery when the SON of GOD Most High, All-holy, All-glorious, hung upon the Cross in mortal agony, naked, bleeding, dying, in the lowest extremity of affliction and suffering, GOD manifest in the flesh, enduring death, even the death of the Cross.

Great was the mystery, when He arose from the sepulchre, in His spiritual immortal Body, ready to ascend, still perfect Man as well as perfect GOD.

But greatest of all, and most full of glory, when the time was fulfilled, and the throne on high was prepared, and the crown was ready, and the multitude of the heavenly host lifted up the gates of heaven, and the LORD JESUS ascended from this earth, and went up through all the ranks and orders of Angels and Archangels, and was lifted up above all the thrones and dominions and principalities of Heaven, till He came to the throne of the majesty on high, even to the throne of the FATHER, when He received all power in heaven and in earth, and was crowned with all honour and glory, most high in the glory of GOD the FATHER. Then they began to sing the new song in heaven itself, "*Worthy is the Lamb that was slain, to receive power, and riches, and wisdom, and strength, and honour, and glory, and blessing.*"

This is the vision of exceeding glory to which we should lift up our thoughts at this season of the Christian year. For now, as S. Paul writes, "*we see Jesus, Who was made a little lower than the Angels, for the suffering of death, crowned with glory and honour.*"

He Who once was laid in the manger, *He* Who once hung on the Cross, even *He*, the same LORD JESUS, is now sitting on the throne of the FATHER, most highly exalted in the infinite power and majesty of the Eternal Godhead. This is the crown and the consummation of the great mystery of godliness, *God the Son made for ever Man, received up into glory,* even into the glory of the FATHER. Now we see GOD our SAVIOUR, no longer in weakness, no longer in suffering, but reigning above in glory on the throne of the majesty in the heavens. Now we run with patience the race that is set before us, *looking unto Jesus, the Author and Finisher of our faith, Who, for the Joy that was set before Him, endured the Cross, despising the shame, and is set down at the right hand of the throne of God.*

If then we celebrate the memory of the lowly *Nativity*, when the LORD from heaven was born into our human family, how much more should we rejoice at the triumphant *Ascension*, when He Who came down from heaven to take our nature upon Him, to suffer and to die for us, was so highly exalted in our nature and ascended to the throne of His glory, far above all creation. If we remember the manger, the cross, and the grave, *how much more* should we remember the throne of glory?

But now let us consider *the exceeding great and precious promise* which the ascended and glorified SAVIOUR of the world sends down to us by His beloved Apostle S. John in the text, "*To him that overcometh will I grant to sit with Me in My throne; even as I also overcame, and am set down with My Father in His throne.*"

Surely this is a promise of such exceeding glory, that we can scarcely venture to think of it. *All* the promises of GOD are indeed exceeding great and precious, but *what shall we* say of THIS? It is so bright and dazzling, that we can scarcely venture to lift up our thoughts to behold it. As the sun in the sky, so this promise in the Bible, is so exceeding bright and glorious, that we can scarcely bear to look upon it.

Our SAVIOUR, on His ascension into glory, does not forget us whom He has left in this world. Although His life of humiliation here below, all His poverty, pain, and suffering have ceased, and He rests above on His throne of glory,—yet He does not forget *one* passage of His human life on earth, He is still perfect *Man*, as well as perfect GOD; He still calls us His brethren, for as soon as He was risen from the dead, He sent this message to His Disciples, "*Go to* MY BRETHREN, *and say unto them, I ascend unto My Father and your Father, and to My God and your God.*"

And does not a true and loving brother desire to impart of his own riches and glory to his poor and needy brethren? If the LORD has been pleased to *make* Himself and to *call* Himself *our Brother;* if He has created and made us for Himself; if He has redeemed us unto Himself with His own most precious Blood; if He has given even *Himself* for us;—how shall He not *also* with Himself freely give us *all* things? how shall He not give us *a share in His own glory* in the world to come? If the LORD, the Creator of all the worlds, has made even one sun in the sky so bright and dazzling that we are not able to lift up our eyes to look upon its glory—how much more will He *glorify His saints*, the dear purchase of His own Blood! how much more will He make *them* vessels of honour, powers full of GOD; shining as suns of glory in the Kingdom of His FATHER; partakers of His own Joy, sharers of the glory of His own throne, reigning with Him for ever!

Still we must all feel most deeply, when we look at our own most utter unworthiness of this exceeding height of Divine glory, that here is a promise of GOD, *so very bright and dazzling*, that we can scarcely bear to lift up our eyes to behold it: "*To him that overcometh will I grant to sit with Me in My throne, even as I also overcame, and am set down with My Father in His throne.*" It seems *too much, too great* a height of glory. Must we not draw back, in confusion of soul, and say with the good centurion in the Gospel, "*Lord, I am not worthy.*" When for our sins we only worthily deserve to be punished, when we only deserve to be trampled under foot by the devils in hell, yet to be lifted up into the glories of the Kingdom of the Incarnate SON of GOD, to be *set before His Face for ever—what* can we say? *what* must we feel? Is it not almost *more* than our little faith *is able to bear?*

And yet we must not think scorn of the promises of GOD, as the unbelieving Israelites did in the wilderness of temptation. The promises of GOD are given us, in His Holy Word, that they may be embraced by our faith, that they may dwell in our hearts, and move our whole being, and stir the very depths of our soul. The promises of GOD ought to be *exceedingly precious* to us. We should ponder them deeply in our hearts; we should live by faith in them; we should depend upon them, as the very rock of all our comfort and hope. As the Israelites of old, in their forty years' journey through the great and terrible wilderness, ought to have been supported by faith in the Promised Land, *that good land which flowed with milk and honey*—even so *we*, in this little period of our mortal life, ought to be living by faith in GOD's word, and preparing for what is coming. For GOD has called us to His Kingdom and Glory.

Do you value, then, brethren, *the Promises of God?* Is your heart lifted up above the trifles of this present moment, and fixed on those things which GOD has prepared for them that love Him? Have you any true ambition, or are you contented with what this world can give you? Do you value life and happiness and glory? Should you like to be a *king?* Should you like to ascend a *throne?* Should you like to live for ever, *reigning* in the midst of Eternal Glories? Do you wish to enjoy the glorious creation of GOD, ever more and more, to all eternity, in the boundless realms of beauty? Do you value life and glory together with Him

Who is the Fountain of all life and glory? Do you desire to receive from Him full torrents of felicity for ever and ever; to rejoice in *His* Presence and in *His* Love, who for your sake laid down His Life that He might lift you up to His own Throne of Glory?—Then lay hold, with all the faith you have, on this Promise of GOD: for here is something which exceeds all that you can desire; "*To him that overcometh will I grant to sit with Me in My Throne; even as I also overcame, and am set down with My Father in His throne.*"

But this, you will say, is *so exceedingly bright and dazzling*, that we cannot well bear to look long upon it. Let us, then, now turn away from the *Promise*, and in conclusion fix our attention on *the condition* which is joined to it. We must never forget to consider *the conditions* which are joined to *the Promises* of GOD. In the present case, *to whom* is the Promise given? Let us mark the words: "*To him that overcometh, will I grant to sit with Me in My Throne;*" the condition is, "*to him that overcometh.*" Here is *a throne of glory* promised; but here is *a battle to be fought* first. The *Crown* is not promised before the *Cross*. What soldier is honoured with a triumph before he has fought in the battle, and *overcome?* What gold is purified without the furnace?

Did the LORD Himself ascend to the throne of His glory before He was crucified? Was *He glorified* before He was tempted and had overcome? Was the great Captain of our Salvation exalted with great triumph into Heaven before He had been made perfect *through suffering?* So it is for all His disciples, in one degree or another, in one shape or another. The Promise of the triumphant Ascension to the throne of glory is given only " *to him that overcometh.*"

What then, brethren, have we all *to overcome?* We have to overcome *our own selves:* " *If any man will come after Me, let him deny himself.*" Here is a great part of our battle—to learn to *overcome ourselves.* And again, it is written, " *If ye live after the flesh, ye shall die; but if ye, through the Spirit, do mortify the deeds of the body, ye shall live.*" We have, therefore, to fight against a part of our own selves, to deny our own wills. Unless, through the HOLY SPIRIT, we learn to do this, we shall die in our sins; we shall never, never be fit to ascend to the throne of glory. We have to overcome, also, the strong hold that *this present world* has over us; for, "*if any man love the world the love of the Father is not in him;*" and "*this is the victory that overcometh the world, even our faith.*" By faith in things unseen but eternal, by faith in the SON of GOD,

Who loved us and gave Himself for us, we must overcome the power of this present world, and learn to live for what is coming. And then we have also to withstand and to overcome the assaults of our great Tempter, as our LORD Himself did; "*Resist the devil, and he will flee from you.*"

At our Baptism, when we were enlisted into the army of CHRIST our LORD, called to be saints, made inheritors of the Kingdom of Heaven, it was on this very condition, that we should fight against, and, *through His Grace,* overcome the world, the flesh, and the devil.

This, then, is our *life-long battle.* We cannot take possession of the Heavenly Canaan without fighting for it. The Israelites in the wilderness forfeited their inheritance, and came short of the promise of GOD. We can never reach the throne of CHRIST our LORD, unless in His Grace we now learn to withstand and to overcome the world, the flesh, and the devil. The promise is only "*to him that overcometh.*" O let none of us think about the throne, if we draw back from the battle!

BY THE SAME AUTHOR.

SERMONS ON THE CHIEF ARTICLES OF THE CHRISTIAN FAITH. Fcap. 8vo., 6s.

"A cycle of sound and well-balanced theology, full, thorough, and systematic in substance."—*Guardian.*
"A sound and judicious volume."—*Christian Remembrancer.*

A SHORT ELEMENTARY TREATISE ON THE HOLY EUCHARIST. Fcap. 8vo. 2s. 6d.

TRACTS ON CHURCH PRINCIPLES. 1 to 12, cloth, 1s. 6d.

"WHAT MEAN YE BY THIS SERVICE?" Some Account of the Meaning of the Chief Service of the Christian Religion. 4d.

THE TYPES AND FIGURES OF THE OLD TESTAMENT. 1s. 6d.

QUESTIONS ON THE CHIEF TRUTHS OF THE CHRISTIAN RELIGION, for Higher Classes. 3d.

QUESTIONS AND ANSWERS ON THE CHIEF TRUTHS, for Lower Classes. Third Edition. 1d.

LETTER TO THE METHODISTS. Second Edition. Price 2d.

PRAYERS AND HYMNS FOR SUNDAY SCHOOLS. Price 2d.

CATECHISM OF THE CHURCH. New Edition. 4d.

CATECHISM ON THE TWO CHIEF TYPES OF HOLY BAPTISM. 2d.

www.ingramcontent.com/pod-product-compliance
Lightning Source LLC
Chambersburg PA
CBHW020923230426
43666CB00008B/1544